Anchor Your Love

10 Date Nights to a Deeper Connection

Shree Prabha

Clever Fox® PUBLISHING
Chennai • Bangalore

CLEVER FOX PUBLISHING
Chennai, India

Published by CLEVER FOX PUBLISHING 2025

ISBN: 978-93-6707-665-1

Contents

Acknowledgements

First and foremost, I want to thank you, dear reader, for choosing this book. Your desire to learn how to improve your relationship is reason enough for me to write it. I hope that you gain meaningful insights and have fun as you read it.

This book was born from my deep belief in the power of connection. Over the years, my clients have affirmed time and time again that relationships are the cornerstone of a fulfilling life. Each session with them has been a revelation for me too, shaping my understanding of what it takes to build relationships that thrive. Their courage, honesty, and willingness to grow and be vulnerable have inspired every page of this book.

I couldn't have written this book without you, my cousin and editor, Supra Varma. Your unwavering support and the countless hours spent refining it have been the backbone of this journey. You egged me on with thoughtful feedback and encouragement and gave me the strength to keep going—I truly couldn't have done this without you.

To my lovely daughters, Sneha, for the hours spent reading and re-reading the book and offering a perspective that sharpened the book's relevance, and Shrishti, who inspired the writing of this one.

I'm deeply grateful to my beta readers, Shashi, Lavanya, and Dhaval, for their time, insights, and invaluable feedback.

To my friend and fellow therapist, Smitha, thank you for championing my wish to write and cheering me on. And to Hari, my friend, your belief in my voice and gentle insistence that I don't trivialize my ideas were pivotal in bringing this book to life. When I said that I didn't know what

I could say that wasn't already said, your words – "The way you say it will appeal to some people and benefit them," – kept me going.

A special thank you to my mom, whose pride and joy in this endeavor has been a constant source of motivation. Your faith in me, even before the book was completed, means more than I can say.

Finally, to my clients – thank you for trusting me with your stories and allowing me to grow alongside you. You have not only shaped my practice but also taught me profound lessons about connection, love, and resilience. This book is, in many ways, a reflection of all that you have shared with me.

My heartfelt gratitude goes out to everyone else that I may not have mentioned, who has been part of this journey.

Thank you all for helping me bring this dream to life.

Overview

Ever feel like relationships are a rollercoaster ride? One minute you're on top of the world; the next, you're hanging on for dear life. Most of us are on this same wild journey.

Imagine holding a roadmap that doesn't just guide you on this journey but helps you build the very foundation of your connection. This book is that navigational compass – a comprehensive exploration into the heart of relationship dynamics.

When you sense the honeymoon period is waning, you start to ponder important questions: What can truly anchor your relationship? How can you build a connection with your partner that gives both of you the freedom to grow? How can you and your partner align your desires and work towards them together? That's the journey this book aims to guide you through.

When exploring relationships, the first person you confront is yourself. There's always a flutter of unease when an insight hits too close to home. You're turning pages, and suddenly, it's as if someone's wiped clear the foggy mirror of your life. Every facet of your personality comes into sharp focus, which can be unsettling. The emotions you've tucked away in the recesses of your mind now take center stage. You might wonder – Do I want to confront all that?

But here's the thing: these moments of clarity and insight? They're relationship gold! Every "aha!" moment, every revelation, builds towards something greater. They're the keys to cultivating relationships that don't just survive but thrive!

Why Couples Therapy?

Relationships are tough. Being kind, honest, and loving isn't always easy. In romantic relationships, this gets amplified a hundredfold. Physical intimacy creates deep bonds that make everything more intense – both the challenges and the rewards. These connections test us like nothing else, bringing incredible joy but also some real heartache.

As a therapist, I've seen couples grapple with complex issues. Relationships need more than just better communication or behavioral tweaks – they need alignment. A thriving relationship isn't just about personalities; it's about understanding that both partners have responsibilities – not just to each other but to themselves as well. True commitment means showing up, even when it's the hardest thing to do.

Therapy aims to create a safe space where couples can dig deep, break free from limiting beliefs, and grow. Couples therapy is not just about two people but also the intricate dynamic they've created together. Through my extensive work with couples, I've realized that most relationship problems don't come from a lack of love. Instead, they stem from not knowing how to take a step back and become aware of the dynamics of the relationship itself.

What Makes A Relationship Work?

Today, relationships are fluid, shaped by personal choices rather than rigid traditions. This freedom allows flexibility with what "works" in a relationship.

Interestingly, ancient traditions also reflect this diversity. For example, in ancient India: Radha and Krishna were eternal lovers who never married; Arjuna eloped with Subhadra; Draupadi had five husbands; Dhritarashtra, Rama's father, had three wives; Shikhandi transitioned from female to male and married a princess; and Shakuntala and Dushyanta married each other simply through a verbal agreement.

These stories remind us there's no single "right way" to love – relationships have always been shaped by context, culture, and individual choices.

In today's age, this fluidity sometimes creates confusion as society balances old norms with new freedoms. However, when both partners are genuinely invested, they can navigate these complexities together and create a relationship that works for them.

Why I Wrote This Book

I've seen so many wonderful people struggle in their relationships, even when they have the best intentions. Just a few therapy sessions can offer clarity, helping them understand each other's thought processes, leading to compassion and kindness. Having experienced my share of love, heartbreak, and betrayal, I know how life-changing a good relationship can be. This kind of insight would've been invaluable to my younger self.

This book is my way of spreading happiness by addressing what causes unhappiness in relationships. Think of it as shining a light on the darkness of misunderstanding and ignorance.

My approach to couples therapy comes from decades of study and personal experience with the mind, spirituality, and human connection. Over 30 years as a spiritual counselor, coach, and therapist have taught me one key truth: Fulfilling relationships are built when partners see each other as collaborators, not owners or gatekeepers. True support begins with taking responsibility for our own emotions, actions, and choices.

The goal is to foster awareness rather than prescribe long and step-by-step processes. I hope this book feels approachable – offering insights that you can reflect on and incorporate into your daily life. It's not directly informed by clinical research or analyzed data but distilled from years of working with couples and universal truths about relationships.

Final Thoughts

This book is for anyone looking to build or nurture a meaningful romantic partnership. Whether you're starting fresh, facing challenges in an existing relationship, or simply looking to deepen your connection, I hope you find valuable insights and tools within these pages. Relationships aren't always easy, but with intention, awareness, and mutual effort, they can be immensely rewarding.

Wishing you love, joy, and connection,

Shree

How to Use this Book

The best way to use this book is together with your partner. You can either share a copy or each have your own. Every chapter begins with a story, followed by insights and exercises, and some space for you to journal. Some of you may enjoy reading the story together, while others might prefer discussing just the insights. Approach the book with an attitude of play and curiosity rather than trying to fix something wrong or find the "right" answer. Reflect on the insights individually first, and then come together to discuss them as a couple.

Enjoy the process! Grab a drink and some food, and make it a date night activity for at least 10 weeks. See if you can connect the story to the insights, and approach the exercises as opportunities to explore new ways of connecting. Most importantly, take your time with it – growth in relationships is a journey, not a race!

The Relationship Wheel

Through the story in this book, we'll explore 10 key aspects of relationships that shape how you and your partner connect and grow together. But before we dive in, let's take a moment to reflect on where you currently stand with a simple yet eye-opening exercise.

The wheel below has been divided into ten key areas that shape any relationship. For each area, rate where you stand by circling a number from 1 to 10. For example, you might feel very unhappy about how you resolve conflicts and rate it a 4/10, while your commitment may be an 8/10. It's not about accuracy but about your perception. Encourage your partner to try it as well so you can compare perspectives.

These are the 10 key areas:

1. **Personality types**: How well do I know and understand my partner's qualities?
2. **Healthy Boundaries**: How well do I set boundaries and respect my partner's needs?
3. **Long-Term Purpose:** How clear am I about what I want from this relationship?
4. **Communication**: How well do I communicate with my partner? Do I feel heard and understood in our conversations?
5. **Interdependence**: How well do I balance my independence with mutual support?
6. **Conscious Love**: How much effort am I putting into showing love to my partner?
7. **Trust**: How much trust exists between us? Do I feel secure in this relationship?
8. **Conflict Resolution**: How well do we handle disagreements? Are we resolving conflicts healthily?
9. **Commitment**: How committed am I to making this relationship work, not just emotionally, but through actions as well?
10. **Intimacy**: How deep is the intimacy in our relationship? Do I feel emotionally and physically connected with my partner?

This exercise will give you a clear picture of your perception of your relationship!

Once you've circled all 10 numbers, connect them in the adjoining sections to form your unique wheel. You'll now notice that a new wheel has formed inside the outline, Maybe one that's uneven – but that's okay! This visual will help you see aspects of your relationship that may need more attention.

Let's Mark Your Wheels!

Partner 1

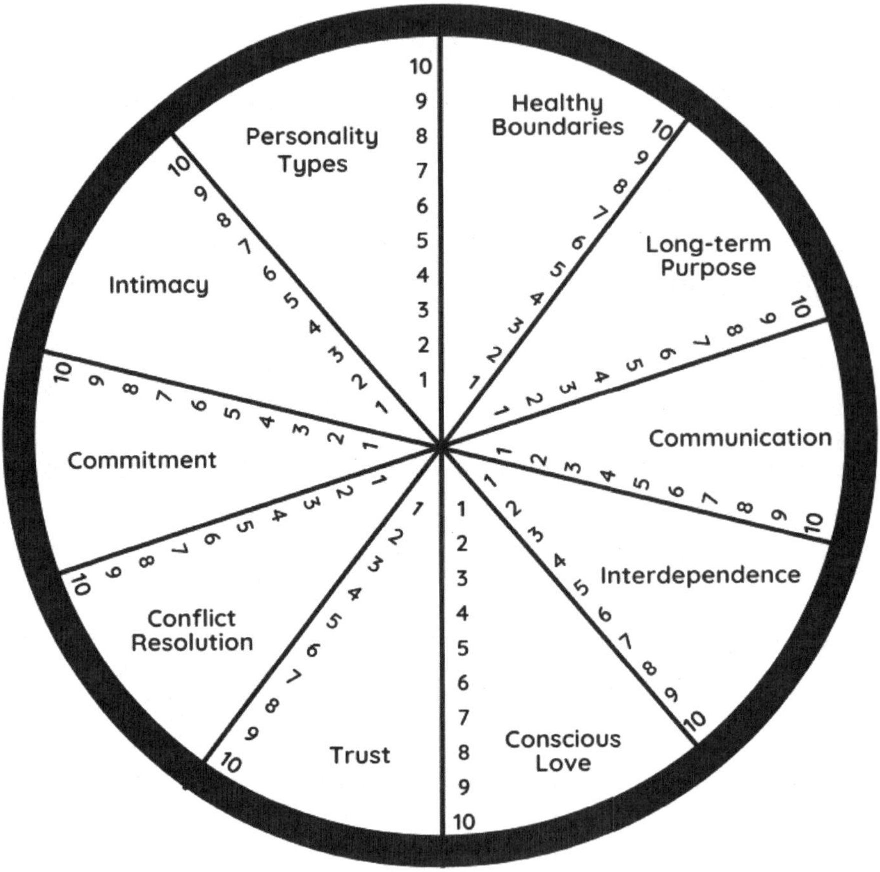

Partner 2

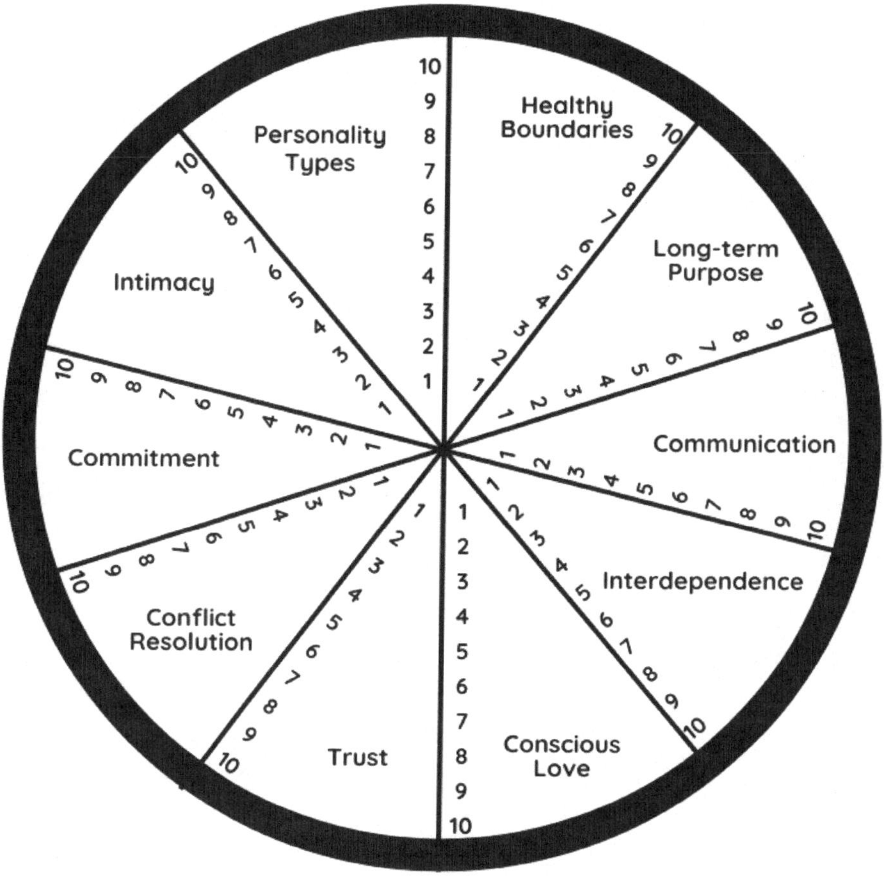

Take a moment to compare your wheel with your partner's and discuss your perspectives. If these were the wheels of a motorbike, how smooth do you think the ride would be?

We'll revisit this wheel toward the end of the book. It will have changed!

CHAPTER 1

PERSONALITY TYPES

The winners of the Lark competition were being announced! Anya waited with bated breath, anticipation filling every pore of her being. The evening was beautiful - artistically hedged gardens framed by a perfect starry night, lilting music playing softly in the background, the aroma of fragrant flowers mingling with the attendees' perfumes.

All of this was lost on her. The large open space, at the most beautiful resort she had ever been to, had shrunk in size and now seemed to occupy only the space of the brightly lit podium.

Anya had poured her heart into this competition. Her video submission showcasing the work done to counsel women married to men with addictions had been intelligent and impactful, and while the response had been positive, her competition was fierce - Arya's video on unemployed graduates and Yen's witty take on advertising gimmicks had won equal acclaim. The prize felt like everything she had ever desired. She really wanted to win.

Anya turned to look at Arya. He was at the food stall, chatting away with the other contestants, clearly enjoying the perks of being a participant. Yen, on the other hand, stood by the beautiful painting of Chammo Lam

Lha, a goddess riding a golden bee. The Tibetan people believed that she could ward off impediments and dangers on journeys.

Maybe he was asking for her blessing on the prize? She thought. He, too, had his eyes fixed on the podium, his usual chatty self nowhere in sight.

"And now, we have our two finalists," said Ankush, the host of the event, with excitement in his voice. "Our mission is simple – to help people discover their own country through travel."

Pausing for effect, the excitement in his voice contagious, he continued, "Lark is like a dating app for travelers. It has been designed to help you discover and travel to interesting places across India with others who share your passion for unique travel experiences. Lark is all about avoiding the usual tourist spots and instead diving into the rich heritage and culture this country has to offer."

Waiting for the applause to subside, he smiled at the audience and announced, "And now, without further delay, the winners of Lark's video-making competition are… Anya and Yen! Congratulations!"

Clapping enthusiastically with the crowd, he continued, "This lucky and talented duo will travel to different towns and villages across southern India, vlogging their journey throughout. It will be an all-expenses-paid adventure where they'll have complete freedom to choose both their destinations and their mode of travel. We hope their vlog will inspire all of you to travel and discover new places with others you meet on our app!"

Ankush then gestured toward the winners and said, "Let's welcome our winners up on stage. Anya, Yen, come on up and accept your prize!"

Amidst the crowd's cheers, Anya walked gracefully towards the stage. She wore a beautifully embroidered green *kurti* paired with stylish cigarette pants that gave her a chic, modern look while accentuating her Indian curves. Yen, smartly dressed in a pair of jeans and a white shirt, bounded up the steps and held his hand out for her.

"Thanks, but I'm fine," said Anya, frowning at the inherent gender acknowledgment in the gesture.

Why the rebuff, Yen wondered as he shrugged it off – *I was only trying to be polite.* Still, it was good to be able to enjoy this victory together.

After all the hands were shaken and the photographs were taken, they were led to a nearby room to meet the founders, Trisha Rao and Kiran Joshi. Trisha, a software engineer who strongly believed that people thrive when they are in tune with nature, and Kiran, who believed that experiences were more enriching when shared with someone else, met at an entrepreneurial workshop. They bonded over their love for adventure and soon left their corporate careers behind to create Lark.

Kiran had an imposing persona and towered over Trisha as they stood up to greet Anya and Yen. Trisha came forward, smiling in welcome, holding both her hands out for simultaneous handshakes. The warm gesture put them at ease immediately.

"Congratulations! We're so excited to have found the two of you," she said. "Anya, I loved the way you show the conflicting emotions in the women and Yen - you were insightful while still being funny, very cleverly achieving the goal of your video. We were looking for creativity and novelty, and you both achieved that perfectly. Well done, both of you!"

Turning to Kiran, she said, "I'm confident that they'll help us launch Lark successfully."

"Hello and congratulations!" Kiran said in a surprisingly soft tone. "Trisha and I have really enjoyed setting up this company, and we can't wait to see how you two will take on our vision and bring it to life. Friendships are born through shared experiences - we hope traveling to new places and creating memories along the way will be a life-changing experience for both of you."

Smiling at this, Trisha said. "It started that way for us, too. The best moments of our travels were when we took the time to meet locals in their own homes. Right, Kiran?"

Kiran glanced at her and laughed, "But you should have seen Trisha's face when they served us some of those strange meats!"

"Well, you had an edge because of your background in hospitality," Trisha retorted competitively.

"We went on so many constantly evolving, completely unplanned trips. It really pushed me out of my comfort zone," Kiran said to Anya, chuckling. "But the enthusiastic and decisive Trisha made everything a lot easier." Anya could tell that Kiran had a deep fondness for Trisha.

"Ankush will go over the details of your travels and plans. Kiran and I wanted to spend some time with you so that you could get to know us and our goals for the business." Trisha said briskly, now getting down to business.

Kiran added, smiling, "And also so that *we* can get to know *you* – and what you hope to do. Ah, here he comes now – our vibrant man Friday! Guys, meet Ankush."

Ankush walked in, full of energy. "What a fantastic opportunity for you both!" he exclaimed, slapping Yen on the back and hugging Anya.

"Honestly, there was a moment when I almost ditched my job to join the competition for a chance to win the prize," he whispered conspiratorially to Anya and Yen.

Yen started feeling a little out of his depth. This was a serious chance, and he felt a bit like an imposter. He brushed the thought off as fast as it came. "I can't wait to get going!" he said.

"So," Ankush said wistfully, "it is not just the places we want you to document or their culture and food. We want people to see how you connect with each other and also with people from all those places. I am sure it's going to be fun to watch how you two get along." he winked at Anya. "Traveling with a stranger and discovering places and people will make the journey memorable - I'm sure it'll be an adventure!"

"How are you feeling about all of this?" Trisha interjected, looking at Yen, and before he could reply, she added, "To truly capture the spirit of traveling 'on a lark,' we want you to travel randomly, making up your journey as you go, embracing the unexpected! I hope you'll enjoy that."

Yen grinned, "I am beyond excited – Happy as a Lark!" he said, winking at no one in particular.

His smile was infectious, drawing returning smiles from everyone. "The unpredictability is what makes it so thrilling. I've never won anything like this before, and all of this is going to be so much more fun with the beautiful Anya around. Thank you so much for opening this door - I plan to run right through it!"

Anya looked at him and wondered. *Beautiful? Is that all he sees?*

Sensing that Trisha was waiting for her to say something, Anya spoke up. "Thank you for trusting us with taking your business forward. I am so keen to start. I can't pretend to know what's in store, but as Richard Branson puts it – say yes to amazing opportunities and figure out the rest as you go!" Anya sounded so sorted.

She paused for a brief second before continuing, "That said, I have to admit, the idea of traveling randomly does feel a bit daunting. I'm just hoping we can work well together and make this journey a great one."

"What a contrasting yet complementary pair they make," laughed Trisha. "It will be fun to see how that works out," she said, looking at Kiran.

"I'm ready to leave right now!" laughed Yen. "I've always wanted to travel around our country and see its beauty through the eyes of different people. I plan to make the most of it."

There it was again – his desire for beauty! Anya rolled her eyes internally.

After some more light-hearted conversation, Kiran turned to Anya and Yen. "Ankush will reach out with all the other details. Be ready to leave in about two days."

Anya's heart skipped a beat. *Two days? That isn't enough time to plan everything and find someone to take over at work. I'd better get everything in order before I go,* she thought, *both for the trip and for my time away from work.*

"And now, Trisha, let's head toward the dinner and drinks," said Kiran. "Time to go and meet everyone else!" He walked toward the door, leading them out.

How was Yen taking this so easily, Anya wondered as they walked out. She sensed that it only seemed that way. *Everyone here seems to have such interesting personalities, she mused.*

The rest of the evening passed in a blur of music, laughter, and dancing. It was the beginning of a new chapter, and Anya wasn't sure yet what was in store, but one thing was clear – her life was about to change in ways she had never imagined.

INSIGHTS

> *"Let there be spaces in your togetherness, and let the winds of the heavens dance between you. Love one another but make not a bond of love: Let it rather be a moving sea between the shores of your souls."*
>
> **– Khalil Gibran**

Gibran's wisdom reminds us of a timeless truth- that connection celebrates individuality rather than erasing it. When we honor our differences as complementary rather than contradictory, our relationships can truly thrive.

Just as no two fingerprints are the same, no two people are alike. While these differences can make relationships challenging, they also provide opportunities for growth. For instance, Ankush's outgoing personality is a stark contrast to Anya's serious demeanor, just as Yen's carefree charm differs from Kiran's thoughtfulness or Trisha's go-getter attitude. While we easily accept these differences in strangers, it can be harder with partners, leading us to wonder as Anya did – *How can they be so different?*

Each of us is a unique blend of strengths, fears, motivations, and communication styles. No personality type is superior; they all thrive in different contexts and are shaped by a variety of sometimes questionable experiences. The real magic to transforming and enhancing our relationships lies in learning how to relate and communicate with each other.

We've been trying to classify this uniqueness for millennia, yet no one has been able to answer what exactly makes us so different from each other. Assessment tools like DISC, MBTI, and the Enneagram give us insight into our minds and behavior, going beyond genetics, culture, and environment. While these tests are usually a journey of self-discovery - allowing you to discover your motivations, communication styles, and even what career might suit you best - they can also be a fun way to learn more about your partner!

However, trying to categorize a partner's persona will only get you so far. It might be wiser to use these assessments as a starting point to understand your partners' unique traits and tendencies and not as a definition or label.

Human behavior, however, isn't set in stone. Life is full of changes, and life situations like trauma or loss can cause significant shifts in our personalities and behaviors. Who you are today doesn't necessarily predict who you'll be tomorrow. A successful relationship thrives when we navigate these differences with awareness. Practically, this means that we create compatibility by acknowledging our differences and allowing room for change.

Acknowledging differences

Acknowledging your partner is like being a mirror -reflecting their image without any changes. It means that you see your partner as they are, with acceptance, and without judgments. This causes a huge shift to take place, because you are saying, "I see you and understand that you are different from me and that is ok". By removing the stress of having to meet expectations, you're creating a sense of safety - and it feels a lot like love.

In addition, you are telling them that you want to be with them after seeing who they really are. Such acknowledgment can completely dissolve defensiveness and allow an authentic relationship to form.

Differences in a relationship can be a wonderful source of growth. Our perspectives can expand to include ideas that would not have occurred to us before. We get forced to challenge the belief systems we took for granted and begin to appreciate how different strengths can make our partnership more wholesome.

> *"What we seek most in our relationships is the freedom to be ourselves in the presence of another."*

Creating Compatibility

What if these differences could strengthen our connections? Compatibility isn't about being similar to your partner but about living well together and it is rarely organic. It is the art of taking your differences and molding them so that your life feels balanced and fulfilled.

Think of ink meeting paper and creating a story neither could do alone-compatibility is created in the same way. When we understand our differences and have a shared vision of where we want to go, we can align with our partners in a far more dynamic way.

Ravi and Khushi, illustrate the dynamics of differing personalities in a relationship.

Khushi enjoys quiet time at home with hobbies like reading and painting. She likes to take her time to get things done as perfectly as possible. Ravi, on the other hand, thrives in social settings – he loves parties and meeting new people.

The couple was elected to host a community *Diwali* celebration. Ravi was quick to whip up a tentative plan and was excited about the project. But when they discussed the details, tensions flared. Khushi noticed several shortcomings in Ravi's plans and felt frustrated that he wasn't listening to her concerns. Meanwhile, Ravi criticized her for taking too long to express her thoughts.

Khushi being detail-oriented was worried about things going wrong, while Ravi's attitude was to just dive in saying, "Let's just have a good time." When these differences weren't addressed or accepted, misunderstandings and emotional distance developed. To fix this, they took the time to understand each other's ways of thinking and learned how to work together by leveraging each other's strengths.

Ravi worked on making the celebration fun and Khushi on making it memorable and inclusive.

Through consciously making these adjustments, Ravi and Khushi can create a relationship that respects both their personalities. This approach fosters acceptance, understanding, and shared experiences, transforming their relationship into a unique blend shaped by their willingness to adapt and support each other.

Activity Time

ROLE CALL - the who's who in a relationship

This simple Activity is designed to help you and your partner recognize and appreciate the unique strengths and differences you bring to your relationship.

How to do this activity:

1. **List the Roles: In the table below is a sample list of roles. You can use these or create your own based on your lifestyle.**
2. **Establish Ground Rules: Agree that this exercise is not a judgment of your partner's character but rather an exploration of who might be a better fit for each role. Feel free to establish any additional rules to ensure that this is fun for you.**
3. **Assign Roles: Discuss which of the roles you believe you will excel in as well as which roles you think your partner would excel in. Remember that we all have strengths in different proportions; for example, I might be good at party planning, but my partner might excel at it and enjoy it more – making him the ideal choice for that role. Have fun with this process and take the time to validate and acknowledge each other!**
4. **Integrate the Story: For more insight, you could also determine who might be the best fit based on the story.(optional)**
5. **Reflection: After completing this activity, take some time to think about how you can leverage your strengths within your relationship to make your life smoother.**

Here is a list of possible strengths listed by role in case you need help deciding.

Role	Strength 1	Strength 2	Strength 3
Party planner	Takes charge	Naturally organized	Efficiency
Host	Warm and welcoming	Caring	Comforting
Creative decorator	Imaginative	Unique touch	Engaging
Budget manager	Detail oriented	Meticulous	Practical
Problem solver	Identifies issues quickly	Analytical	Decisive
Logistics of travel	Resource management	Researcher	Time management
Negotiator	Persuasive	Insightful	Confident
Home organizer	Methodical	Practical	Thoughtful
Wellness coach	Encouraging	Goal oriented	Supportive
Handyman/woman	Mechanical skill	Curious	Learner
Idea generator	Innovative	Resourceful	Drives growth
Peacekeeper	Mediator	Gentle	Listener
Morale booster	Validating	Compassionate	Boost confidence

Which of you is a better fit?

Role	I think the best fit for this role is: (me/my partner/ us)	Because it requires (xyz skills)	From the story – who would fit best?
Party planner			
Host			
Creative decorator			
Budget manager			
Problem solver			
Logistics of travel			
Negotiator			
Home organizer			
Wellness coach			
Morale booster			
Idea generator			
Peacekeeper			
Handyman/ woman			

"We all should know that diversity makes for a rich tapestry, and we must understand that all the threads of the tapestry are equal in value no matter their colour."

– Maya Angelou

Journal Time

Takeaways from this chapter

Use this space to jot down your thoughts and responses. I have added some questions to help with this. You may use them or not- but do write! When you come back to this after a while it will strengthen your understanding and the resolves you made.

Me

What did I learn about differing personalities? How do I usually approach differences in personality types?

My Partner

How is my partner different from me? What assumptions do I hold about him/ her?

Our Relationship

How does embracing the uniqueness of my partner enrich our relationship? What can we do to be more accepting of each other?

CHAPTER 2

HEALTHY BOUNDARIES

The two days had flown by.

Anya had had a hectic two days. She'd handed over her work to different colleagues and informed her bosses about the three-month sabbatical she was taking. While they didn't like the idea, they didn't want her to quit either. There had been a lot of resistance at home, too. Her parents didn't get why she wanted to take time off from her career to travel and "find herself."

"You can find yourself here – within your work," they had said. They also had a lot to say about her "gallivanting around the country with a strange man and no concrete plans". Anya, being in her late 20s, was frustrated at having to gain their approval.

"Why are you so determined to prove yourself in ways that don't matter?" they had questioned.

"It matters to me!" she'd snapped, rolling her eyes. "And the fact that you're asking me is exactly why I'm doing it."

When am I going to be treated like a grown-up? She thought. Anya packed quickly and sensibly - emergency supplies, her journal, comfortable yet sharp clothes - and left.

Yen, on the other hand, had it easy. He lived with four other single working men in a shared house, and this trip was a welcome escape from the chaos. His roommates had no sense of personal space, constantly leaving their belongings everywhere, throwing late-night parties, and finishing up all his food. A break from the daily grind sounded perfect to him. After informing his boss and his roommates about his decision and tossing a bunch of his clothes into a bag, he was all set to go. His mother was very pleased that he was pursuing something he truly enjoyed.

Anya and Yen were to meet for breakfast at a café near a train station before heading out. They were to meet Ankush so he could hand over their gear and answer any last-minute questions.

Yen, who hadn't factored in extra time for the morning rush, reached right as Ankush walked out the door. "Time, man, it's one of the biggest reasons for conflict," Ankush said with a smile. "All the best to you both, and remember – I'm just a phone call away in case of emergencies."

Yen walked in and hesitated, seeing Anya's displeased frown from the door. "I hope we'll be able to respect each other's time during this trip, Yen. I feel a little fussy about it" she said, holding up her fingers to show how much –a tiny bit, but enough to make a point.

"Hey, I didn't foresee the traffic, sorry!" he apologized, quickly deflecting "Let's go! Come and take a selfie with me – to mark the beginning of our journey."As she leaned in to pose for the picture, smiling at the camera, they felt like a team for the first time.

I'm gonna win her over, thought Yen.

Anya and Yen had agreed to start the journey with a trip to a village in Kerala. "Let's get our minds and bodies ready for the journey," she suggested. "Rejuvenation before endeavor is a perfect idea," he agreed.

I hope that sounded smart, he thought. *She isn't easily impressed!*

The train arrived early in the morning, leaving them a short bus journey away from the Ayurvedic village they planned on visiting.

Kerala, mused Anya, sitting by the window of a rather empty bus*; it's called God's own country, and the reason is not hard to see.*

Sun baked houses nestled within lush green landscapes, rich & fertile soil stretched between swaying coconut trees while the crisp, unpolluted air gently carried the scent of damp earth and foliage. She took a deep breath and smiled, feeling content with how her life was unfolding.

Yen, on the other hand, was focused on the clean, winding roads and the simplicity in everyone's demeanor. He glanced down at himself, somewhat self-conscious of his bright, colorful clothes. Still, they both readily agreed on how leaving the bustle of the city behind for this was an extremely refreshing and necessary change of pace.

The bus rounded a corner, and the centre loomed into view. Tucked away in a forest and bordered by towering mountains, it looked like the perfect place for a detox, complete with modern facilities, wholesome food, organic farming, herbal gardens, and yoga and meditation centers. They were greeted warmly and handed refreshing herbal drinks before being given a tour of the stunning property.

There was a large fence that ran all around the property "It's important to demarcate lines well," their guide explained. "We need them to maintain the quality and produce of our products. Inside this space, we're free to do what we want."

"In the evening," he continued, "our oldest Ayurvedic doctor will be giving a talk. Please do attend; he is an excellent speaker and has years of experience to draw from. Everyone gathers when he speaks- it might be a great way to connect with the locals and our residents."

He then showed them to their rooms. Anya could see the forests and the mountains from her balcony, while Yen's room had a view of the gardens and the farms. "Between us, we've got all the views covered," winked Yen.

After changing into comfortable clothes and enjoying their simple vegetarian dinner, they walked to a central courtyard where about 50 people had gathered. At the front of this group was a man in his seventies wearing a white *mundu* and shirt. A long, flowing white beard hid most of his face, but his eyes were alert, and he spoke in a deep baritone voice.

"Ayurveda developed by observing and learning what sustains each type of life. We are all interconnected, and it's the same life energy that flows through us all. However," he said, pausing to make a point, "it flows differently in each person. Even though we're all made up of the same basic elements, they are molded uniquely, which is why our bodies function differently. By living a disciplined life with healthy eating and sleeping habits, we can keep our bodies balanced. All we do here is to restore that balance so the body can heal itself," he explained.

Yen looked around at the gathering and was struck by the wide range of ages among the listeners. Young teens were just as focused on the speech as people in their sixties. There seemed to be a general sense of love and respect for the speaker.

How does someone become so profound and be able to influence so many people? He wondered.

His mind drifted to his own life; growing up in a home with a single mom, he could never shake off the idea that his father had left them. He'd often questioned whether it was because he wasn't enough to be around for. It made him constantly look for validation from the people in his life. Now, he couldn't help but wonder if he'd ever be able to command the same kind of respect and admiration that the speaker had earned.

Anya noticed that he was lost in thought and nudged him. "Listen," she said, gesturing towards the doctor, "this could help us understand everything here better."

Yen tuned back into the talk. "Each one of you is unique, with your own mental, physical, and spiritual essence. That's what makes you, you! When life pushes you away from your innate nature, or when you try to be someone you're not, your body feels a sense of unease and, in the long run, ends up diseased. This is why you must make time to know yourself and care for your body. Here in this village, we want to give you the space and support necessary to know and accept your body and mind."

Sitting amidst the intense quiet of the surrounding forest, listening to the sage speak, and having enjoyed a nourishing meal, Yen felt a profound sense of peace. He turned to look at Anya, who seemed completely absorbed in the discussion. She had a steadiness about her – something that made him feel like he could turn to her for direction.

She noticed him watching her and smiled. They had started developing a bond from just the thought of experiencing time, places, and people together.

"I'm heading back," Yen whispered to Anya. "Enjoy the rest of the talk." She nodded, mouthing back a "Good night!"

The next few days were wonderful. They woke up before dawn and followed a morning routine, focusing on self-care and setting intentions for the day. They participated in yoga and meditation sessions and attended several talks and lectures on the ancient science of Ayurveda.

During their free time, they walked up natural hiking paths, visited a nearby village, tended to the herbal gardens, and learned how to cook Ayurvedic meals. They usually ended the day journaling and sharing reflections. They had begun to notice how nurturing and caring for themselves and others in the village uplifted their mood and energy, and how the relationships they formed seemed so smooth and effortless.

Anya had started to appreciate having Yen around. He was at ease talking to anyone and everyone, and always left people with a smile on their face.

His spontaneous plans seemed ridiculous but ended up making every experience more exciting. She smiled as she recalled the way he had jumped into a lake they had stumbled upon. She would never have done it herself if it weren't for his enthusiastic pleas and happy laughter.

"Shall we figure out our next destination?" Anya said one evening. She had just wrapped up her part of the vlog and was going over the footage to make sure she had everything she needed. Yen was standing behind her, watching.

"Maybe you could make it a bit more light-hearted?" he suggested as he watched her vlog. "Thanks, Yen, but that's your style. I'd prefer it if you gave me feedback when I asked for it. When you're hovering over my shoulder, assessing my work, I find myself unable to work. I've mentioned this before." Anya turned to look him in the eye.

"I'm sorry, Anya," said Yen. "You're right. As the speaker said the other day, there is just unease when we interfere in each other's work. I'll wait until you want to know what I think. But I do have to say, seeing you work so diligently is inspiring," Yen smiled to himself. He liked the way she guarded her work.

"Thanks, Yen," she said, smiling to say it was okay. "By the way, you look pretty great in these videos."

Was that a compliment or a declaration of attraction? Yen wondered.

"Well, let's see how much better we can do in the next location," he said, with what he hoped was a smile of confidence and charm.

An hour later, after a bit of back-and-forth, they had picked their next stop- the towns surrounding the city of Madurai. It was a perfect blend of ancient traditions and long-forgotten stories and they were excited to go.

INSIGHTS

> *"Before I built a wall I'd ask to know, What I was walling in or walling out, And to whom I was like to give offense."*
>
> **– Robert Frost**

In his poem "Mending Wall," Frost explores deliberate and thoughtful boundaries rather than arbitrary demarcations. He contemplates questions such as: Who will I let in and to what extent? Will my boundaries create distance or offend?

There is a delicate balance between individuality and togetherness in relationships. As Anya and Yen travel and evolve, they subconsciously reflect the teachings of the Ayurvedic doctor they met. Both are becoming more at ease with themselves and each other, accepting and honoring their differences while retaining their unique essences. For instance, Yen felt comfortable leaving a meeting in which Anya was engrossed.

In many relationships, there's an unspoken expectation to do everything together. It leaves one partner feeling pressured to 'adjust' or 'give in' and sacrifice their own needs. Compromise, turning a blind eye, and prioritizing your partner has traditionally been viewed as the foundation of a good relationship. While this may have worked in the past when dependencies were common, today's reality is quite different. Each person is capable of sustaining their own life, and what we seek in a partner is someone who adds value to our lives. Modern relationships demand mutual respect and individuality.

> *"We don't want our partners to complete us anymore; we want them to enhance us!"*

The lines that we draw to say what is ok and what is not, is key in maintaining balance in healthy relationships, much like the balance emphasized in Ayurvedic healing. Ayurveda views illness as a consequence of imbalance. Similarly, when boundaries that support a person's emotional and physical well-being are crossed, unhealthy relationships form.

Understanding and Communicating Your Boundaries

Defining boundaries starts with a key question: *What can I allow in my relationship without compromising my well-being?*

Boundaries are the lines we draw between ourselves and others to define the limits of our interactions. Just like the walls of a room or the borders of a country, boundaries create personal spaces – areas where we feel comfortable and safe.

Having a clear sense of who you are and what matters most to you is essential both to establishing your boundaries and to giving your partner the freedom to do so too. When we have the perspective of "I'm okay, and you're okay", boundaries become acceptable.

Understanding that a boundary is not about shutting out your partner, but rather defining what makes you comfortable, can make it easier to accept your partner's boundaries as well. Therefore, it is key to develop the ability to articulate our boundaries and recognize when they are being tested or crossed.

For example, when Yen interrupted Anya's work, she firmly asked him to respect her time and focus without being offensive. By expressing her needs without anger, she prevented a small issue from escalating into a battle of wills.

"While it seems counterintuitive, caring for yourself is a prerequisite for being able to care for a relationship"

The Importance of Boundaries in Relationships

When boundaries are valued, you are communicating respect and trust. Open communication about boundaries fosters healthier relationships, by providing clarity to your partner about what is important to you. They protect your physical and mental well- being and prevent feelings of being used or taken advantage of.

Completely sacrificing your own needs for the sake of a relationship may feel easy in the moment but can quickly become a cause for regret. Relationships where this is the norm don't last, and even if they do, they leave partners feeling frustrated or resigned to a life of unhappiness. Not managing boundaries effectively can lead to conflict, resentment, and even abuse, because disregarding needs becomes acceptable.

Maintaining individuality within a relationship becomes important because it allows each person the space to breathe and grow.

Boundaries aren't just about saying "no." They are primarily about maintaining your comfort and integrity in any setting. Establishing and communicating your boundaries can help to create a healthier dynamic that respects both your needs and those of others.

Let's look at a couple of examples.

Consider a child who is asked to hug an uncle or aunt when they don't want to. Adults may insist on the hug, brushing aside the child's discomfort in favor of "politeness". This could lead to the child learning that their boundaries don't matter and their feelings can be dismissed. Imagine how much confusion this could cause when the child grows up.

Similarly, let's consider the example of an adult in a workplace break room, where a casual conversation suddenly turns into office gossip. He finds himself trapped, feeling increasingly uncomfortable but unsure how to exit gracefully. He feels internally conflicted - Should he leave and risk being seen as antisocial? Should he speak up and take a stance? Should he just keep quiet and look for a way to leave at the right moment? In such scenarios, it becomes important to learn how to enforce one's boundaries gracefully and with tact.

The Spectrum of Boundaries

Boundaries, like many aspects of human interaction, exist on a spectrum. Their effectiveness lies in striking a delicate balance. When boundaries are too rigid, they can lead to isolation and when they are too weak, they can cause distress.

Rigid Boundaries: These are unyielding boundaries. While they definitely help in certain situations and can protect us from harm, if they're applied all the time, it can lead to a perception of coldness. For example, saying no to drunken driving every time is a good boundary, however saying no to partying always because it's a waste of money might be too rigid. Rigid boundaries that are not useful usually stem from a history of trauma, abuse, or neglect.

Porous Boundaries: In contrast, porous boundaries are easily crossed. This often occurs when we prioritize pleasing others at the expense of our own needs, driven by a fear of rejection or an excessive attachment to someone. Such boundaries can leave us feeling used and resentful. In a relationship where emotional sharing is easy, having porous boundaries can allow for intimacy but also cause overwhelm.

Healthy Boundaries: The ideal lies somewhere in between. Healthy boundaries are flexible enough to allow for compromise while still protecting our needs and values. They foster an environment of respect and safety. For example, a work from home partner can say," While I am happy to take on extra responsibilities around the house, because I don't commute, I still need my work time respected."

Establishing Boundaries

People often cross boundaries simply because they aren't aware that they exist. This is usually an unintentional error. For example, if you prefer to pay for your food on dates but your date insists on paying without asking you. This only becomes a breach if they continue after you express your discomfort.

Consider another scenario: if your partner feels comfortable discussing private issues openly with friends, but you prefer to keep those matters private and have communicated this, yet they persist in sharing – this becomes a violation of your boundary.

Teaching others how you want to be treated is a good skill to have. While these conversations can be challenging, they are necessary for the health of your relationship. Open and safe communication about boundaries helps create mutual understanding and respect, leading to stronger connections.

Practical understanding

Let us look at some of the areas of life that are important to the well-being of a relationship and see how boundaries function in each of those areas.

Type of Boundary	What it is about	Example of breach
Physical	• Your Body • Your Resources • Physical Distance from another	• Assault • Smothering with affection
Intellectual	• Your beliefs • Your opinions • Your need for privacy	• Dismissiveness • Invalidation of your thoughts • Questioning your beliefs in public without reason.
Conversational	• How much you want to be involved • Not sharing personal information if you don't want to • What you are willing to discuss	• Forced to share reactions and feelings • Having to discuss politics in a gathering when you don't want to

Time	• Showing up on time • How much you're available to another • Taking personal time	• Working overtime without compensation • Inability to say no to invitations • Having to attend parties because it's a family thing
Material	• Money • Possessions	• Taking without asking • Expecting financial support
Sexual	• Your safety • Your sexual preferences	• Not listening to a no • Touching without asking
Emotional	• Availability to listen • Self-regulation	• Having to be a sounding board even when tired

Building a great relationship involves forging a delicate balance: we must know ourselves while also finding strength in sharing with our partner, all without losing our individuality.

Partners need to thrive together both as individuals and as a team.

Activity Time

COLOURED FENCES

Here's an interesting activity to let you discover boundaries that you and your partner have and how you respond to them. The first table serves as an example, while the second table is for you to fill in with what's relevant to your own relationship. Feel free to make your list as long as you like! Afterwards, compare notes with a spirit of curiosity. You might be surprised at how easy it can be to be inclusive rather than dismissive.

Boundary area	What makes me uneasy	What makes my partner uneasy	How I feel about my partner's boundary	How can I accept their need?
Finances	Spending without a plan	Having to ask for money	Why is it so hard to ask when we love one another?	Come up with a plan to have a basic sum of money easily accessible.
Time	Being late for appointments	Their time is taken for granted	Isn't it a given that in a relationship time is of essence?	By asking rather than expecting.
Sex	The unsaid expectations	Having to talk about sex	I get it- it's the upbringing	Sign up for a couple's intimacy workshop

Our boundaries

Boundary area	What makes me uneasy	What makes my partner uneasy	How I feel about my partner's boundary	How can I accept their need?

"A good marriage is one in which each partner appoints the other to be the guardian of his solitude."

– Rainer Maria Rilke

Takeaways from This Chapter

Any journey that is inward needs time and space for self-reflection. Use this space to jot down your thoughts and responses. Please use these questions to guide your thought but don't limit your reflections to just answers!

Me

What boundaries do I need to feel safe? Where do I struggle to set or maintain boundaries?

My Partner

How does my partner set boundaries? Do I respect their boundaries even when it makes life difficult for me?

Our Relationship

How will drawing boundaries affect our relationship? What can we do to communicate our boundaries so that it strengthens our connection?

CHAPTER 3

LONG-TERM PURPOSE

"The world is so interconnected," Anya said as they drove through the Western Ghats early the next morning on their way to Tamil Nadu from Kerala. Pointing to the side, she asked, "Did you know that this gap in the mountains is mirrored in the mountains of Madagascar? Millions of years ago, we were all part of a single landmass that broke apart and drifted off," she said, gazing into the distance.

Yen looked at her dreamy face and chuckled. Anya had a vivid imagination and often got lost in her thoughts.

The lush greenery and gushing waters they encountered had a stilling effect on him. The huge rock formations, trees growing at impossible angles, and the sight of steep drops ironically gave him a sense of grounding and safety. Traveling with Anya was a completely different experience. It was so unlike his usual trips with friends – which involved music, dancing, drinking, and sometimes being in a haze from the high of psychoactive substances – yet he was surprised to find this style of travel equally enjoyable.

They stopped for a while at a roadside tea stall, drinking warm *chai* and gazing at the mountains in companionable silence.

"I've always focused on doing things that would lead to some kind of success, you know? This is the first time I'm doing something purely for the joy of it." Anya said, suddenly feeling reminiscent. She took another sip of her tea and, noting Yen's attentive gaze, decided to continue.

"My mom's quite a famous endocrinologist. She consults at the top hospitals in the city. And my dad's a banker. They've both set such a high bar for achievement and sometimes I wonder if I can ever be like them," she said, sighing. "My sister is a lot younger than me - still in college - and intent on following in my dad's footsteps. She loves the fast pace and the ambition of the corporate world, and wants to make a name for herself"

"And what about you?" asked Yen. "Why did you choose your career?"

"I started studying psychology because I wanted to understand how people think and feel and how that shapes their lives," she said, her voice drifting off slightly. "But when I began practicing, I realized just how complex our minds are. Theories capture just a few aspects of it." She paused and then smiled.

"This is the first time I've traveled without family or friends, and honestly, I'm so glad we get along so easily. I have my own space, but I still get to enjoy this experience with you – it's perfect!" She sighed, feeling a sense of peace. Yen no longer felt like a stranger, and she found it easy to talk to him.

Yen leaned back in his chair and stretched his hands as he reflected, "The hustle and bustle of a city comes with its plusses, but it seems like the calm and quiet of these places speaks to you more, isn't it? Have you ever thought of what you truly want in life?" He paused to look at her before continuing. "It takes tremendous courage to choose, though. I think that's why we so often just dream about what could be."

Anya shrugged and nodded. "The grass is always greener on the other side."

Then, giving her a half-teasing smile, Yen asked, "Do you have any secret dreams about where you want to live and with whom?" His eyebrows were raised playfully, but there was a hint of seriousness in his question. He found himself wondering about the possibility of them being in a serious relationship.

"Secret dreams are not meant to be shared," she laughed, heading back to the car. "They are meant to be cherished -secretly!"

Soon, they passed through the villages in Tamil Nadu. They decided to avoid the highway to better understand how the local people lived.

The residential areas seemed so welcoming, with intricate designs drawn on the floor in front of houses. "*Kolams*," said Yen, "that's what they call them here."

"It's an art form, *thambi*," said the driver. "In the early morning, the lady of the house will clean the front of the house, sprinkle water all around, and sit down to draw these."

"It's amazing that such intricate designs are drawn knowing that it's just for the day. Even though the wind will blow it off and passersby will step on it, so much care is put into each one," said Anya.

"Ah, but the rice flour used to draw the *kolam* feeds ants, squirrels, and small birds; it's a way of living in harmony with the surrounding nature," said the driver.

"The Tibetan monks do something of this sort in their temples, spending hours creating a beautiful drawing only to erase it when their work is done. There's a video of it, I'll send it to you," interjected Yen.

The driver wasn't done yet. "Her mind stays focused because the process is so detailed. It's a meditative way to start your day. She creates beauty and calms her mind," concluded the driver. He spoke in Tamil mixed with some English, but both of them understood him perfectly.

They saw a rather large *kolam* being drawn and stopped to watch and take videos.

"One slip and the design goes for a toss," explained the woman, her hair tied back in a knot and sari tucked away to give her the freedom to move and draw. "The patterns are made with simple dots, lines, and curves, but they also need symmetry. I have to stay focused on what I want it to look like at the end."

Finishing with a satisfied smile, she stood up as she surveyed what she had done. "It's good for both the body and the mind," she said. Seeing Anya and Yen's attentive faces, she asked, "Would you like to stay and have breakfast with us?"

Yen nodded enthusiastically, beaming. Anya too smiled, both at the woman and at Yen's exuberant reaction.

What amazing warmth toward absolute strangers, thought Anya. *It's amazing how she has managed to be meticulous and planned while also being so spontaneous.*

Back in the car after a delicious breakfast, Yen was elated. "The food was finger licking-ly yummy!" he said. "I think I've just found my new favorite breakfast. It's going to be *idlis* every day here – nothing beats Tamil *sambar*!" He couldn't stop raving about the hospitality, the family, and the incredible food.

"Relationships are a lot like the *kolams,* don't you think?" mused Anya. "A tangled web of emotions and actions. And just like them, if we don't pay attention, everything can get messed up"

How is she able to think so deeply? Wondered Yen. *And here I have been going on and on about the food.*

"And just like with *kolams*, we need to make an ongoing effort every day to nurture a relationship. It can seem like hard work unless there's satisfaction with the effort, I guess," Yen added.

Anya turned to look at him, her eyes wide with surprise, and said, "Wow, Yen! You're right."

The driver was very pleased with the whole experience. "It's been a pleasure to drive you both around. I'm going to buy you both some *kolam* powder, and you can try your hand at it when you are free," he said.

Anya turned to him, surprised. *Again, such lovely warmth from strangers, spontaneously and freely given,* she thought.

"Thank you so much, *anna*. We appreciate your kindness," she said, her voice sincere.

The driver smiled warmly at them, clearly pleased. "It's the little things, you know?" he said. "In this world, it's the simple gestures that make people feel good. You don't need big things – just a little friendliness, and it can help people connect. It's important to do that, and I try to do it whenever I can."

They arrived at Madurai by noon and checked into a modern, comfortable hotel. They had adjacent rooms, overlooking a large pool sheltered from the sun by tall trees all around. One look at it and both of them headed down for a swim. After some fun water races and acrobatics, they returned, laughing and tired, ready for lunch and a long afternoon nap.

Later that evening, they spotted an empty piece of land nearby. Armed with their *kolam* powder, they set out to experiment with some designs.

"What do you want from life, Yen?" asked Anya, laying out neat little dots, trying her best to recollect the styles they had seen earlier.

"I want to experience as much of life as possible. I love my freedom, but I also want to know how to have deep and stable connections with people. You are so good at that," he said.

Anya waited for more, and so he continued, "My parents divorced when I was 14. I stayed with my mom. She's a fierce and outspoken lawyer," he said, his voice full of pride. "She always encouraged me to explore life independently."

Anya was listening to Yen intently. "And what about your father?" she asked.

"Dad visited regularly, but there was always this unspoken tension between them - they both needed to be the better parent. I quickly learned how to please them both, you know, to keep the peace. It's been a useful skill in my work," he said with a dry chuckle.

She reached out, lightly touching his arm. "You are laughing off something that must've been so difficult. Do you still prioritize keeping the peace in your relationships?" she asked her voice soft.

Yen glanced at her. "Who doesn't want peace?" he replied. "I get very nervous around conflict."

Realizing the conversation had taken a heavier turn than he'd intended, he quickly shifted gears. "By the way, your kolam is looking amazing. Almost exactly like what you set out to do, huh?"

He had chosen to draw what looked like a continuous curving line, which he had to redo a couple of times to get right. He looked at hers – it was a neatly done geometric pattern with flowers and a border.

Different ways of drawing, just like there are different ways of living, he thought. They stayed for some more time, trying their hand at intricate patterns and even doing some of them together.

As the days passed, their local excursions to nearby towns and villages opened up a world of stories and perspectives. Filming videos, compiling and editing them, and meeting so many different people kept them occupied and fulfilled. They slowly developed a friendship that was both pleasant and easy.

Their next destination was Araku Valley, a picturesque hill station in Andhra Pradesh, famous for its lush coffee plantations.

INSIGHTS

> *"To the person who does not know where he wants to go, there is no favorable wind."*
>
> **– Seneca**

Seneca suggests that if you are unsure about your direction in life, you cannot accurately determine whether an event is in your favor or against you. This principle applies to individuals as well as couples. As a couple, have you discussed what you want out of being together, or have you left it to chance?

Anya and Yen are developing a friendship based on experiencing life together. A strong friendship forms the basis of any good relationship. Anya has started to be more spontaneous, Yen has become more vulnerable and they have learned to accept each other. The early stages of a relationship can be quite beautiful in this way - building one is a creative process. Certain fundamentals are in place, and there is flow toward the ultimate goal. Initially, that goal is just being with the other person.

Successful long-term relationships demand that both partners continuously work to create and sustain meaningful shared value. Problems tend to arise either when couples lack clarity about what they want or when one partner has different desires and hopes the other will adjust their expectations over time. But, for instance, if one partner wants a child and the other doesn't, there is no middle ground!

In therapy, I encourage couples to look at their relationship as different from themselves - like a separate entity. Think of it this way: if you and another person were starting a business together, that business would have its own identity, distinct from the two of you. One of you might take a logical and analytical approach, while the other might be more intuitive and visionary. Despite these differences, both of you would focus your skills on the common goal of making the business successful. When the aim is to maintain the business effectively, you and your partner work collaboratively. However, if the focus shifts to determining who contributes more or trying to prove the other wrong, the business ultimately suffers.

Understanding the purpose of our relationship and actively working toward maintaining that direction is important. Many of us tend to unintentionally sabotage this whole process due to a lack of clarity about the shared goal.

Let's illustrate this with an example.

Sheila and Arun love each other and are sure they have found something valuable in their relationship. Ultimately, they both desire an emotionally stable partnership that offers companionship.

Sheila works at a corporate firm with regular hours, while Arun is an entrepreneur and is called upon to work at odd hours. As a result, they spend quite a lot of time at their respective workplaces. When they do get together, they usually prefer to unwind by socializing with friends. This busy lifestyle leaves little room for building the companionship that they both seek.

Consequently, they feel empty and experience conflicts about their needs, occasionally even mentioning divorce in the heat of the moment. However, this doesn't align with their true desires at all! How can they achieve stability if the threat of separation looms over them, or expect companionship to flourish in public settings? Even though they know what they want, failing to clarify their shared vision could ultimately sabotage their relationship.

Relationships require conscious effort; they need to be nurtured and course- corrected consistently.

Activity Time

COLLABORATIVE VISIONING

Purpose: To create a shared visual representation of your desired future together.

How to do this activity:

1. **Collect Materials:** Bring out all the material you want to represent your future visually.
2. **Find Your Inspiration:** Spend some time separately searching for words, quotes, or images that symbolise your desires from your relationship. Look at different aspects of it like home, family, travel, personal growth, shared values, etc.
3. **Discuss:** Talk about why you chose certain images or words. Explore how they represent your hopes and dreams for your future together.
4. **Create Your Vision Board:** Put together what you have chosen on a single board. You could also make a collage of different boards. Make it visually appealing and fun!

Reflection:

Notice what themes stand out in your vision board- that is what will keep your relationship thriving. How will you build towards your shared dreams? Also consider where your dreams diverge and address how you will support each other with those.

> *"Alone we can do so little, together we can do so much."*
>
> **– Helen Keller**

Takeaways from This Chapter

Use this space for self-reflection and jot down your thoughts and responses. I have added some questions only to provoke thought. Please use it as a space to journal so that you can come back here later to connect your dots.

Me

Why do I want to be in a relationship? What does having a partner give to my life?

My Partner

What does my partner want from our relationship? Do I align with it?

Our Relationship

How can we create a shared vision that makes both of us feel fulfilled?

CHAPTER 4

COMMUNICATION

Anya had swiveled her seat to face the hills as the train to the scenic Araku Valley wound its way through stunning landscapes of green, sloping hills. The train featured special coaches with large windows all around, including ones on the ceiling, which provided a panoramic view of the journey. In the distance, she spotted waterfalls and tall trees covered in climbing plants, shrubs filling in every inch of available space. Occasionally, she could see the front of the train snaking its way along the tracks.

A slow journey like this, where time feels paused, is such an antidote to the rush of everyday life, she thought. *It has to become a mandatory mental wellness rule for life.*

The kids on the train were full of energy, their excited whoops filling the air each time the train plunged into a tunnel, only to reemerge into the daylight with a chorus of cheers. They were keeping a running tally of their "tunnel adventures". She glanced out at the hills, but her mind drifted to Yen.

Yen had befriended a biker at Vizag and had chosen to ride with him and his group of bikers to Araku Valley.

I wonder how he's faring, she thought. *He's probably whooping, too, hands outstretched with the wind in his hair and whizzing up and down the hills.*

She caught herself smiling at the thought and stopped immediately, pulling herself back to the present.

People around her were discussing their plans for the day since most visitors came to the valley for a day trip. Anya and Yen, on the other hand, had chosen to stay in Araku Valley for a week to participate in a community project that supported the local tribal population. They were going to help with a training program designed to help women create a self-help group for selling local handicrafts online.

Meanwhile, Yen was having a great time with the bikers. They were a group of four friends who had just finished college and decided to travel around India before working. Their journey along the steep bends was filled with cheerful banter and infectious enthusiasm. Yen took in the breathtaking views – deep green valleys, mist rising from the forests, and villages tucked neatly into the hillsides. He was experiencing a visual and mental feast!

Wanting to share this feeling with Anya, he texted her, "There is something about mountain air, I feel so alert and clear-headed."

"It's quite peaceful on the train ride too," she texted back almost immediately.

He smiled at the instant reply and looked up, tucking his phone away. He saw two women who had precariously seated themselves in the trunk of a car with its hood open to enjoy the ride. He waved at them and took a picture.

"See you at the caves!" they shouted, assuming he was a tourist, and pointed at a lone deer that had appeared nearby. Monkeys were everywhere, and Yen's camera was working overtime trying to capture all the wild beauty around him.

Despite all the stunning footage, he felt a pang of dissatisfaction. *Our videos need to do more than just show the place*, he thought. *They need to tell a story*. His eyes roamed over the picturesque mud houses, their thatched roofs blending into the green landscape like something out of a postcard.

They stopped at a coffee plantation to enjoy the delicious hot coffee that Araku was famous for. He had sent a picture of this to Anya. Her reply was playful: "It couldn't possibly compare to Luwak coffee. You know, the one made from the half-digested beans collected from civet poop?"

He laughed to himself, wishing she had come on the ride too.

Due to the various stops along their journeys, both Yen and Anya arrived at their resort at almost the same time. Smiling, they walked toward each other. "Good to see you," they said in unison, followed by a shared laugh. It was becoming an easy and comfortable rapport between them.

A sumptuous lunch and a much-needed siesta later, they decided to stroll around the resort. Cobbled pathways, colorful flowers, rustic benches, and Buddha statues made it seem like any other resort in the country.

"We should live closer to the locals," Anya said, her tone thoughtful.

"And not get to see the beautiful mountain views from the balcony?" countered Yen.

"Well, the views are everywhere," she said. "A homestay might not provide the comforts, but it will be a good way to get footage on more than the views." She knew that's what he wanted too.

"True, but I don't want to rough it out either. Can we wait a day or two before we make a decision?" Yen asked.

"Sure," she said and then pointed at a dog playing with its ball. "There's certainly no difference as far as dog fun goes," she said, smiling, and walked toward it.

The next morning, they woke up early, setting up their cameras in the workshop. A middle-aged man with a white beard and balding head approached them, exuding an energy that was impossible to ignore.

"Hey there! I'm the organizer of the workshop. You can call me Rish. I hope you are ready for the project," he said. He was full of positive and vibrant energy and immediately set the tone for the next few days.

Anya and Yen exchanged looks and then nodded. Rish's upbeat manner would be easy to follow.

"The participants might be a little challenging to get to know. They don't always share their opinions. I've found that listening to their doubts and skepticism goes a long way in opening their minds to learning," Rish said, speaking with an assurance that came from experience.

"Regardless of where we are in the world, the ability to connect and communicate is the most important skill to have" he added.

Soon after, a group of about twelve women entered, dressed in colorfully printed saris, adorned with glass bangles and lovely nose rings. Yen immediately approached them, greeting them and welcoming them with hands folded in a *namaste.*

As Rish started talking to the women about the program, Yen noticed that they appeared very reserved. They listened intently but did not have anything to say or ask. Yen admired the patient manner in which Rish conducted the training, and reflected on his own style of communication.

How does he communicate so patiently, despite the lack of responses? Yen wondered. *There would be a lot to learn this week.*

A woman named Priya, who seemed to be the leader of the group, sat in the very front, occasionally smirking at Rish's attempts to engage the women. Yen, being curious about the woman and their completely alien way of living, decided to strike up a conversation with her.

"Do you not approve of what is being done?" He asked Priya.

"Yen garu, all this… it's of no use. We should be at home, looking after our housework," Priya said, seeming withdrawn.

"Is it because you think it's not practical?" Yen asked, to clarify.

Priya shook her head. "Not like that. People come here; they talk about changing our lives. Everyone wants to help us grow and they also want to show others what they have done here. But it makes no difference to our lives. We go back home and things stay the same," she said.

Yen paused, trying to understand. "So why did you come today?" he asked.

"The lunch here is nice, different from the normal food we eat," said Priya, shrugging.

Yen couldn't help but laugh. "Fair enough," he said. "But Rish is trying to help you make more money so that your lives can improve. Don't you want that?"

"Ha-ha!" she mock-laughed, covering her mouth with her hands. "Any money we make goes to our husbands, who will spend it as they please."

Anya had been listening in and she now interjected, "At some point, we need to decide if our lives belong to us or our families."

Priya looked at her, surprised. "It's easy for city people like you. Look at you, a young woman, traveling by yourself; you are free to do what you want. We can't do that. We have to listen to others here."

"But this trip happened only because I stopped listening. My family too has expectations and conditions," she said quietly, but with surprising intensity. "It is just expressed differently."

Letting the words hang in the air for a moment, she continued. "When we have to break free of norms, all of us need the same kind of courage, no matter where we are from."

Priya nodded in agreement and said, "You're right, ma. It takes courage to get what we want. I'll wait and see how this program goes."

Just then, Rish returned to the room and continued, "We have a solution for your problems, an opportunity for all of you. It is a way to earn more by reaching beyond Araku. Don't let your fears hold you back. Please, take your first step, and let us support you through the process."

Yen looked at Priya and noticed that she was now listening to Rish with interest. He then turned to Anya and said, "I didn't realize your family disapproved of this trip."

"They think I'm wasting my time. They also don't like that I'm traveling around these cities with a stranger."

He put his arm around her then and said, "I've graduated to friend now, haven't I?" She smiled, put her arm around him, and replied, "Definitely so, Yen. I hope you get to meet them sometime."

Teaching the women how to use the internet to market their products and understand finances and seeing how much progress they had made at the end of the week deeply moved Anya and Yen. Priya especially had begun to open up, her enthusiasm spreading to the rest of the group. By the end of the week, the women were ready to start their co-operative and launch their products online.

Yen took many photographs of both the women and their work, while Anya wrote blog posts for them. Rish then combined everything into a stunning website.

The last day arrived all too quickly, and the women decided to perform the dhimsa, a native dance form. They invited Anya to dance with them, and Yen decided to experiment with the drums, creating the beat for the dance. When he looked up to see the women enter the dance space, he couldn't take his eyes off Anya.

She wore a bright yellow *sari*, large snap-on nose rings, clinking bangles and anklets, and flower-adorned hair styled in a bun at the nape of her neck. Despite her reservations, she took her place among them with a shy smile and a determined stance. Yen felt a strange tenderness in his heart.

Anya was engrossed in figuring out the rhythms and mastering the steps of the *dhimsa* dance. Although she was conscious of everyone watching her, she felt happy to be spontaneous and to have stepped out of her comfort zone. From the corner of her eye, she noticed Yen looking at her and smiled to herself.

The one time she had tried being in a relationship, it hadn't ended well. Since then, she had thrown herself into her career and studies, leaving little room for romance. She wondered if this was what it could be like to open her heart again, and found herself warming to the idea.

They were leaving the following day, but tonight was all about dancing and enjoying the local delicacy made with wild mushrooms, slow-cooked rice, and chicken wrapped in bamboo shoots.

"Thank you for all your support," said Rish as the night drew to a close. "This has been a very successful project. You've helped bring real change to these women's lives."

"It's been a privilege, Rish. I'm amazed at how you've ensured that no one gets left behind. I'm so glad to have been a part of this," said Anya.

"At work," she continued, "I don't usually share much about myself, I only focus on the clients. But I've learned now that it is important to give a part of oneself too. Sharing creates openness and allows us to relate to others so much better."

Yen nodded. "I feel the same way, Rish. It's been so rewarding to be part of something that matters. I felt refreshed to be able to openly care."

Anya looked at him, surprised. Yen was not at all what she had assumed him to be. Through the journey, he had become more vulnerable, and more responsible.

The cover definitely doesn't say anything about the book she thought, smiling to herself.

INSIGHTS

> *"The single biggest problem in communication is the illusion that it has taken place."*
>
> **– George Bernard Shaw**

The saying goes, "Assume makes an ASS out of U and ME." Shaw captures this idea perfectly: we believe we've communicated our needs clearly, only to be proven wrong by the consequences of our assumptions.

Have you noticed how good communication can transform relationships? Take Yen, for example. His curiosity about Priya, combined with his knack for listening without judgment, made all the difference. Being genuinely curious opened up the conversation and helped him get to the root of the issue.   Similarly, when Anya shares her own experience, it resonates with Priya and inspires her to respond and take action.

When someone listens to us with genuine interest in our thoughts and experiences, it allows us to open up and we become better able to address any issues we're facing. Equally true is the fact that others listen only when we can genuinely open up.

So-is communication a natural talent or a learned skill? While some are born with the gift, all of us have had to hone it as a skill at some point. But here's the catch: When a skill is learned incorrectly, it becomes hard to change it. The big question we should ask ourselves while communicating is: "Does my way of talking achieve its intended purpose?"

Miscommunication is one of the most common reasons for failed relationships and lingering bitterness. During emotionally charged moments, we struggle to articulate our true feelings, sometimes even expressing the opposite of what we want to. Non- communication too is equally destructive. When our partners don't know what is going on with us, it can create quite a lot of anxiety and reactions based on assumptions. As such, failing to hone communication skills properly can create a lot of problems for a person.

> *"Words carry immense power, and their impact can linger long after a conversation ends."*

Communication is a vast topic that encompasses various skills, including speaking, listening, questioning, and creating safety – all of which play an important role.

Speaking Effectively

I use a simple model called MESH to help people express themselves effectively, especially during important conversations. Once you get used to this tool, it will become second nature and you will find yourself using it effortlessly in all kinds of situations. MESH is an acronym for the four aspects of good communication.

M: Message: The heart of communication

The message is the core of what you want to say. Think clearly about what you want to convey and phrase your words accordingly.

Questions to ponder:

- What am I trying to say?
- What do I want to achieve by saying this?

Example: I want to say that I am hurt by a public remark my partner made about my weight. I want to help my partner understand how I feel and be more mindful of it in the future.

E: Effectiveness: The delivery of communication

Effectiveness is about ensuring that the message is received as you intended. It involves choosing both how to communicate as well as when to do so.

Questions to ponder:

- How should I express myself so that I am clear?
- When is the right time to communicate this?

Example: It might be better to bring up the topic in a private setting rather than to react immediately in public. I will also ensure that my tone is not one of accusation and blame, but assertive.

S: Spark: The reason for communication

Knowing the true reason behind your message can help you respond rather than react. Is the trigger external (caused by someone's behavior or due to some situation) or is it internal (your perception or history)?

Questions to ponder:

- What has prompted this message?
- Why is it important to say this?

Example: I am hurt by the fact that it was a comment made in public (external trigger -partner's behavior).

Or

I am hurt because I have been trying so hard to lose weight and such a comment makes me feel like a failure (internal trigger- based on history).

It is important to bring this up so that my partner understands my sensitivity and such situations don't rise in the future.

H: Hurdles: The challenges in communication

Hurdles refer to the obstacles in communication. It can be physical, psychological or even physiological. Identifying this accurately can help you address it proactively.

Questions to ponder:

- What stands in the way of a smooth conversation?
- What can cause miscommunication?

Example: My partner might dismiss the situation as a joke. Also, my hurt feelings might make it difficult to say what I want, without sounding accusatory. This means that I have to calm down before bringing it up and say clearly that the joke was at my expense.

Karan and his group of male friends had long dreamed of going on a biking trip, and now the opportunity has finally arrived. However, his friends are teasing him about not being able to make any decisions without his wife's consent. Six months ago, he had to cancel a weekend trip with them because his wife told him that she couldn't go as it was too last-minute.

He wants to go on this biking trip, but it coincides with his fifth wedding anniversary. Karan wants to make his wife happy and knows that she is looking forward to a special celebration together. He is faced with the challenge of communicating his desire to go on the trip without hurting his wife or dismissing their anniversary. Here are some ways he might handle this:

A: Karan might say, "I've been slogging at work and need a break. The guys are planning a biking trip. But I know you will want me to stay here because it's our anniversary."

Outcome: His wife is likely going to focus on the 'you want me to stay' and perceive that he doesn't want to be with her, leading to conflict.

B. Karan may also say, "These friends of mine are planning on a bit of fun, but I want to stay with you because it's our anniversary. We can have our fun."

Outcome: This message may be perceived as insincere especially if his wife wonders why he had to bring up his friends at all. It may also leave him resentful about the fact that his friends might be right with their teasing.

C. Another approach could be, "Would you like to spend our anniversary going on a biking trip with my friends?"

Outcome: It sidesteps the real issue creating a further complication if she said yes (it was to be an all male trip). She might also perceive that he was somehow trying to combine his desires without thinking about her wishes.

D: A thoughtful approach could be to say, "I want to celebrate our anniversary together and do something memorable. At the same time, I would love to go on the long-planned biking trip with the guys. I was wondering if we could celebrate our anniversary the weekend before the date, and then I could go on the trip afterward. What do you think?"

Outcome: He has effectively conveyed both his wish to celebrate their special day and his desire to go on the trip, while also addressing the scheduling conflict. This opens up the conversation and can lead to a resolution as he is inviting her input.

Activity Time

MISTAKEN

Since communication is a rather complex and layered topic, this exercise will help you address some of the most common pitfalls in communication.

Start by thinking of three different conversations you want to have with your partner; it could be about extended family, finances, sex, children, travel plans, etc.

Now, express what you want to say in each of the styles listed. As you do so, observe how each approach makes you feel and also how it might affect your partner. Allow them to do the same, and then compare your experiences. (For further clarification, please look at the example below)

1. Accusing
2. Complaining
3. Sacrificing
4. Collaborating
5. Demanding
6. Detached
7. Curious

I have an example for you. Let's say I want to talk to my partner about our financial situation that '***There's never enough money***!'

1. **Accusing**: "You're the one who keeps spending money without thinking, aren't you?" (makes me angrier and makes him disheartened)
2. **Complaining**: "I don't understand why we always seem to be struggling. It's exhausting." (makes me feel helpless and him irritated)
3. **Sacrificial**: "I'll cut back on the things I want so that we can save more. I don't mind sacrificing my own desires." (makes me feel like it is unfair and him like a loser)

4. **Collaborative**: "Can we sit down together and go over our spending? I'd love to find a way we both feel comfortable with our budget." (makes me feel a sense of control and makes him feel supported)
5. **Demanding**: "We need to stop wasting money, and that means cutting down on *your* unnecessary expenses immediately!" (makes me feel like a tyrant and him avoidant)
6. **Detached**: "We're over budget again this month. We need to cut back on something." (makes me feel resigned and makes him also feel resigned)
7. **Curious**: "What's your perspective on how we're handling our finances? Is there something I'm missing?" (makes me feel like we can find a way out and makes him interested in discussion)

As you can see each approach can bring about different responses in both of you.

Effective communication also involves listening, showing empathy, and asking the right questions. This is better learnt in person and I delve into all this in greater detail in a workshop for enhancing communication called EnMesh.

> *"Communication works for those who work at it."*
>
> **– John Powell**

Takeaways from This Chapter

Think about a conversation that went wrong and one that went right. Reflecting on those might make this journaling more personal. Use this space to jot down your thoughts and responses. The questions are meant to guide your introspection.

Me

Am I able to articulate my thoughts, keeping in mind the context? Do I listen to hear or to respond?

My Partner

How does my partner communicate their needs and wants? Do they speak directly or try to subtly say what they want?

Our Relationship

How can we create a safe space that makes both of us feel open to honest communication?

CHAPTER 5

INTERDEPENDENCE

Hurtling toward Hampi in an old auto rickshaw driven by a young man who - apparently - loved to race, Anya clutched her bags and the auto's sides for dear life. Yen, on the other hand, was at ease, laughing and chatting with their driver.

The famous Hampi festival was set to begin that evening, and people were arriving from all over the country – and from other countries too. The excitement in the air was palpable; it felt like Hampi was the place to be for the next few days. Artisans loaded their vans up with drums, masks, and larger-than-life puppets while villagers from surrounding areas filled up their booths with colorful, unique goods. Hundreds of brightly dressed onlookers filled the streets, adding to the joyful chaos.

Given the huge influx of visitors, Anya and Yen were lucky enough to find rooms. The small, simplistically furnished rooms were a stark contrast to what they had experienced so far, but the exuberant atmosphere left no room for complaint.

Anya was excited about the elephant processions and the art exhibits that showcased tribal art. Meanwhile, Yen was excited about the theatre performances and the road shows featuring the mythological stories of the Ramayana. They found a schedule and tour map of Hampi at a local restaurant, where they had gone to have a late lunch.

"Let's go see the elephants," Anya said excitedly "I've heard so much about how the mahouts decorate them, and I absolutely love elephants!"

"Of course! After that, we should visit the ruins and the temples. The architecture there is breathtakingly beautiful!" replied Yen.

"I'd love to sit with the artisans showcasing tribal art and learn more about their work," Anya added.

"And I'm hoping to watch the processions and the larger-than-life costumed figures. I want to interview the troupes and see how they pull it all together," said Yen.

As they talked, it was clear that they were both interested in different aspects of the festival. Initially, they tried a plan that included what they both liked, sacrificing some individual interests. But later they decided to spend this day doing all the things they both enjoyed and split up the next day into everything else. It would make for an interesting video too if they showcased how two people could enjoy the same events in such different ways.

The evening was a blur of activity. They admired the ruins and temples, took in the mix of people and animals flittering about, and ate as much street food as they could. At the end of the night, as they sat under the stars watching a light-and-sound show and listening to stories of empires past, Anya and Yen felt a deep sense of togetherness. When it ended, they found a spot nearby, sitting quietly together amid the chatter of people heading home.

Anya was sitting with her back against a stone step, her head resting on Yen's knee, as he sat on a higher step.

I wonder if we are heading into more than just a friendship, thought Anya, glancing up at Yen. *I'd better be careful not to mess up our dynamic.*

Absently, Yen reached out to tuck a strand of hair behind Anya's ear. "Shall we call it a night?" he asked, bending down to be heard.

As she turned up to nod at him, Yen found himself thinking about kissing her. It must have shown on his face because Anya quickly stood up.

It might get complicated if I ask and she refuses, he thought. *Besides, I just ate that pungent chutney.*

He stepped back, feeling a little embarrassed. The walk back to their rooms was a bit awkward, with both of them trying to regain a sense of normalcy.

Anya set off early the next day, her day carefully planned out. Dressed in a comfortable, flowing pink dress and a cap to shield herself from the sun, she resembled the perfect tourist. With her camera slung sideways over her shoulder; she headed toward the ruins. Before heading into the festival, she wanted to walk amidst the temples and the ruins to fully soak in the town's essence.

Spotting a cute café, she stopped for breakfast and met Tarun, a software engineer, who had come from Hyderabad. They sipped their coffee as he excitedly talked about all the aerial shots he was going to get with his drone.

"I can show you how to use this if you like," he offered.

Anya smiled, feeling intrigued. "Yes, I'd love that!" she replied.

As soon as they stepped outside, Tarun took out the drone and began to give her a hands-on demonstration. She waved at the drone as he flew it in their direction and then tried her hand at navigating it.

They then decided to head to the ruins together and spent a fun time getting different shots from various vantage points. When they were done, she invited him, "Come have dinner with me and my travel buddy tonight," she said, adding, "Yen is a lot of fun, and I think you'll enjoy meeting him!" Tarun readily agreed.

She spent the rest of the day exploring the art stalls, talking with various artisans, taking pictures of them and their beautiful artwork, and recording their stories. The Lambadi women stood out with their vibrant, colorful clothing – an explosive blend of threads, shells, mirrors, and even coins. She sat for a while with them, quickly learning the basic embroidering stitches.

"Take this," said one of them giving her a small pouch, "So that you remember us!"

"Thank you! I'll buy some of your bags too, to share this memory with others back home," she replied, to their delight.

The elephant procession was later in the day, and Anya arrived early to grab a prime spot by the railings. As the magnificent creatures approached, she was captivated by the elaborate, colorful designs covering their faces and trunks – a display of traditional artistry that turned the procession into a moving canvas.

Kolams for the face and body, she mused, smiling as she remembered trying her hand at the *kolams* with Yen.

Meanwhile, Yen had headed in the direction of the performance artists. He hadn't thought about what he wanted to do and so wandered around the town, talking to the locals and eating at some stalls. As he approached the performance area, the busy preparations for the procession caught his attention. He readily joined in their labors and they offered to let him walk in the procession with them for a while; He took some time to learn how to maneuver one of their giant processional figures by walking inside it.

Nice to look at, but it's so hot and stuffy inside, he thought. *It's impressive how much people give to their crafts.*

There were drummers, dancers, and performance artists all around, creating an electric atmosphere of shared excitement. Yen caught sight of Anya in the distance, engrossed in talking with a group of people as they waited for the processions to start. She looked pretty in her dress, he thought, taking a picture to show her later.

For dinner, they had chosen to meet at a local open-air restaurant, known for its delicious dishes. Yen was surprised to see Anya seated with someone else and deep in conversation.

"Hey," Yen said, sliding into the seat next to her. "What a day it's been!"

"Hi, Yen!" Anya smiled, her face lighting up. "This is Tarun. He's a techie from Hyderabad. Tarun, this is Yen – the one I've been telling you about," said Anya, introducing them.

"What did she tell you?" Yen enquired playfully, as he reached out and shook Tarun's extended hand. "All good things, I hope!".

"Absolutely! And now that I've met you, the description is confirmed," Tarun chuckled. "So, have you two been together long?" he asked.

"Not long enough," Yen replied with a wink at Anya. "But I'm sure we'll get there."

"Long enough to know that it's never going to be boring with him around," said Anya. "Never!" she added for emphasis.

"Aww," Tarun said with a grin. "Nothing like new love, huh?"

Anya and Yen looked at each other, shocked and caught off guard by the comment.

Quickly shrugging it off, Yen laughed and asked, "So, what brings you to Hampi, Tarun?"

"I'm cataloging all the festivals of India," he said. "I have a video channel dedicated to it. I'll send you the link!"

"I'd love to see it," said Yen, smiling.

"How was your day, Yen?" asked Anya, also deciding to overlook Tarun's comment.

Yen's face lit up as he recalled the day's events. "It was amazing. I even joined the elephant procession. I walked right past you, Anya. I was the green giant that tipped toward you!"

"Hahaha, I remember that!" she laughed. "It's amazing that you could just join them like that!"

"The camaraderie among the troupes was lovely," Yen added, his voice softer now. "I've never felt so at home with strangers before. For that matter, I haven't felt so at home, even at home! It felt good to join in their preparations."

"And how was your day, Anya?" he asked, looking at her inquisitively.

"I had a fabulous day too," she said, her eyes sparkling with excitement. "I took some amazing drone shots using Tarun's gadgets, learned how the Lambadi embroidery bags are made, and met a lot of talented tribal artisans!"

"To decorate everything the way they do is such a celebration of themselves and their homes. They haven't tried to be trendy and minimalistic. I like that – the unapologetic way of being what they are!" she said. "I also bought some bags for my sister and mom," she added, sighing. She was beginning to miss home.

"I saw you standing with the women earlier and got a pretty good shot," said Yen. "It should be on your phone."

"I got it," Anya replied, "I had to wrestle a bit to get that spot. Didn't want to miss a thing," she added with a light chuckle.

"How nice this is," declared Tarun. "Perhaps this is the best way to travel; each person doing what they want and bringing back different experiences at the end of the day!"

"Well, we did make time for fun together as well," Yen said. "I think that's what makes it so special."

"It is ideal!" Tarun added after a moment's thought. "My girlfriend and I tend to do everything together, even when one of us isn't too keen on it. It sometimes leads to a bit of resentment," he said with a sigh, leaning back in his chair. "Anyway, I'm heading back tomorrow. Time to get back to the grind of my real job!"

The three of them spent the rest of the evening exchanging stories about their day, laughing and enjoying the moment.

This feels like home too, Yen though. *Perhaps home is just where I can feel belonging and can be myself.*

Anya, on the other hand, was missing her home. She was used to stories around the dinner table and this moment took her back to time spent with her family.

INSIGHTS

> *"I can never be what I ought to be until you are what you ought to be."*
>
> **– Martin Luther King, Jr.**

While this quote may initially seem to focus on two separate individuals blossoming into their true selves, it subtly, and quite beautifully, highlights how achieving this growth requires interdependence.

Ever wondered how some couples manage to stay close while maintaining their identities? Both Anya and Yen enjoy their independence, free from resentment or fear of spending time apart. They take this a step further by sharing their separate experiences and perspectives. Their bond deepens because each has had the space to explore their interests. They even inspired Tarun to try the same with his girlfriend.

Independence doesn't necessarily create emotional distance in the same way that dependence doesn't create intimacy. Many couples lose their spark when they don't give each other space. Some older couples who have become habituated to doing everything together, for instance, can start to seem like siblings. Familiarity causes them to gradually lose the chemistry that once fuelled their connection.

Of course, when you're just starting to like someone, allowing your partner space to do their own thing can feel challenging, especially if there's insecurity. The fear that the relationship may not continue or the urgency to get it to a stable place can cause us to let go of ourselves, starting a pattern of dependence.

Couples who grasp these differences find they're able to navigate the complexities of their partnership without sacrificing their individuality.

Let us look at this in some more detail.

Dependence

There is nothing wrong with relying on your partner to meet your physical and emotional needs. While this initially gives us a sense of intimacy and togetherness, taken too far, it can lead to unhealthy expectations and a loss of individuality. If you did not grow up with the freedom to be self-reliant, then dependence feels normal. When insecurity or loneliness drives dependent behavior, it can result in partners feeling resentment and frustration.

Independence

The other end of the spectrum is independence, where one partner may become so self-sufficient that the other feels excluded or unwanted. When practiced in moderation, independence allows both partners to grow personally while still being in a relationship. However, excessive independence usually arises from fears of betrayal, past experiences of unreliability, or cultural norms that equate being independent with strength. This extreme can create emotional distance, causing partners to miss out on the joys of their relationship.

Interdependence

Interdependence is a healthy way of being dependent or independent. When you understand your inherent value, you can see the value of another person sharing their life with you. It should not be confused with the idea of co-dependence, which is the state of slowing unhealthy dependence. Interdependence becomes a safe space where partners can experience both dependence and independence without tilting unhealthily in any one direction.

How these tendencies form

Our childhood experiences shape how we participate in adult relationships – you can only relate healthily with others when you feel secure within yourself. For instance, if a child grows up receiving support and affirmation while also understanding that there are boundaries that she shouldn't cross, she learns how to ask for help and offer support healthily.

On the other hand, children coming from more dysfunctional homes grow up learning to manipulate others for their own needs. This causes a constant swing between dependence and independence that can destabilize relationships.

Understanding these dynamics is a game-changer for relationships. Sometimes imbalanced behaviors are caused by past trauma and can be detrimental to a relationship if we are unaware of them. But when we can safely talk about it in a relationship, we learn the best way to hold space for letting the patterns heal. It allows partners to give and take in a meaningful way without feeling depleted.

In my experience, couples tend to feel a lot more secure when they each maintain their personal lives, which they can then share with one another. Having unique passions and interests adds a spark to our lives, and it's important to remember that a romantic relationship thrives only when there is an "other" with whom to share it.

Satya and Daniel found themselves sitting in their therapist's office, having had frequent arguments where neither felt like their needs were being understood. They had very different approaches to connection. Satya was deeply dependent on Daniel, constantly seeking his approval and reassurance. She would frequently call him, even for simple decisions like what to cook for dinner, constantly asking for his input. Having grown up learning to please others, she believed that Daniel wouldn't feel loved if she didn't include him in everything.

In contrast, Daniel prided himself on being independent. In his upbringing, vulnerability was seen as a weakness, so he dealt with his problems alone and made plans assuming Satya would just follow along. He rarely shared his emotions with her, thinking he was being strong for her sake. Instead, this left Satya feeling ignored and unimportant.

Their relationship began to unravel because of these differences. Satya complained that she felt neglected and left out of Daniel's life, while he felt suffocated by her constant need for reassurance.

During therapy, as they discussed their fears, Satya admitted that she was terrified of losing him if she didn't keep him updated about everything. For the first time, Daniel paused to reflect on this and realized that her dependence stemmed from fear. He then opened up about his fear– that leaning on someone would make him appear weak and threaten his identity.

Once they both understood that their issues weren't caused by each other but rather by their fears, they decided to learn how to connect in a way that honored both of their needs. Satya began exploring her interests independently, while Daniel started sharing his struggles with her and leaning on her for support. This shift allowed them to grow closer while respecting each other's needs.

Activity time

The three-way balance

Here is a simple activity that you can do with your partner to see how you can balance the polarities of independence and togetherness in your relationship:

Step !: Create your circle of interests

1. Draw a circle and divide it into three sections. (Write as many details as you can think of under each section)

- Your own interests: Section 1: Write down all the activities you enjoy that your partner doesn't care about.
- Your partners Interests: Section 2: Let your partner do the same – let them write down all the interests and hobbies that don't matter much to you.
- Shared Interests: section 3: Write those activities that you both enjoy doing. Perhaps that's what brought you together or how you met.

Step 2: **Experience Your Interests** (spread this over three or four different days or weekends).

- On the first day, spend time doing what you alone enjoy, separately from your partner, Your partner does the same. Meet up later and share how your day went and what you enjoyed/learnt.
- On the second day, do something you both enjoy together.
- On the third day Try out one of your partners interests with them even if you aren't too keen on it. Discuss how this felt
- On the fourth day Let your partner try one of your interests with you and then discuss how it felt

Step3: **Reflect**

Compare these experiences to understand your personal relational dynamics.

What did you find out about yourself, your partner and your relationship?

Here is an example from a couple that illustrates this.

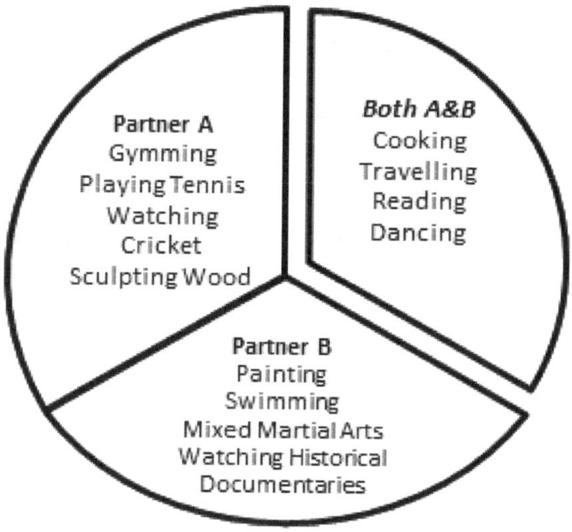

Day 1: Partner A chose to stay at home sculpting wood and Partner B spent the day Painting.

Day 2: Both of them decided to cook a meal and host their friends for dinner

Day 3: Partner A decided to go swimming with B

Day 4: Partner B went to the Gym with A

They decided to continue cycling through their individual interests to keep their relationship fresh and exciting.

> *"Interdependence is a choice only independent people can make."*
>
> **– Stephen Covey**

Takeaways from This Chapter

Use this space to jot down your thoughts and responses. I have added some questions to help with this. Perhaps you could work on some questions for reflection along with your partner.

Me

How well am I able to be myself in the relationship? Am I focused on just myself or just the relationship or do I have a balance?

My Partner

Am I supportive of my partners' independence or do I just want the togetherness? How does my partner feel about our time together?

Our Relationship

What are the habits we can develop so that we have a strong sense of both connection and autonomy?

CHAPTER 6

CONSCIOUS LOVE

"Thank you for agreeing to come to Warangal," Yen said to Anya, "I've always wanted to come and see the architectural beauty it's famous for!"

"I haven't heard much about it, but I guess that's the whole point of this trip – exploration," Anya replied. "But after this, we must visit a city by the beach. I want to kick back, put my feet up, and relax by the sea from sunrise to sunset!" she asserted rather dreamily.

"Deal! It already sounds wonderful" Yen agreed.

They were staying with Ranee, a college friend of Yen's. Her house, by a peaceful lake, felt comforting and welcoming.

"You're both welcome to stay as long as you like," Ranee said with a warm smile. "I live alone, so having guests is a real treat!"

"I've ordered some delicious *Hyderabadi Biryani*, and we've got yummy *chutneys* and pickles too. Hope you're hungry!" she added, raising her eyebrows at Yen.

"Ravenous!" Yen grinned. "She used to bring the best lunches back in college," he said, explaining to Anya.

"I had to pack enough for four!" Ranee laughed. "My mom loved to cook though, so it was never a problem."

Anya sat back as they shared stories of pranks and fond memories from their college days, enjoying the playful banter between Yen and Ranee.

"By the way," Ranee began, turning to Yen, "Do you remember Surya? He's getting married the day after tomorrow. I mentioned to him that you'd be here with a friend, and he insisted I invite you both. I hope you'll join us!"

"Surya is Ranee's cousin," Yen explained to Anya, turning nostalgic "Back in our college days, he used to hang out with us a lot. We were hiking buddies, and he blended in perfectly with our gang of friends."

As memories of those carefree times resurfaced, Yen and Ranee went down memory lane again, their laughter weaving through the room. Turning to Anya, he asked with a playful smile, "What do you think? Would you like to experience a traditional Telugu wedding?"

Anya nodded languidly, "I'd love to!" she said, already imagining the vibrant festivities. Then, with a grin, she added, "It's the perfect excuse to buy a sari from here too!"

Going along with last-minute plans was becoming second nature to her now. Before meeting him, her life had revolved around a meticulously planned schedule, every moment accounted for. Now, she smiled at the memory of a time when they had pulled the stopper on a bus and hopped off just because Yen had spotted a brick kiln and couldn't resist learning more about it. *Perhaps being with Yen makes it easier for me to embrace spontaneity*, she mused.

The next day was a whirlwind of exploration, each stop more awe-inspiring than the last. The temples they visited were masterpieces of craftsmanship, their intricate designs speaking of a long-lost era.

At the entrance to the Thousand Pillar Temple, Yen came to a halt, captivated by the delicate stone carvings before him. "Anya, just look at this detail," he said, his voice filled with wonder. "Every pillar here tells a story. Can you imagine the sheer effort it must have taken to create something like this?"

She smiled, her imagination running with him as he continued. "Hundreds of years ago, in a city most people don't even know exists, a king dreamed of this and brought it to life. It's fascinating!"

Anya reached out, her fingers feeling the cool, weathered stone. She traced the fine grooves of a lotus flower, each petal etched with care by hands long gone. "It's incredible," she whispered. "Imagine the patience it took – like they poured every ounce of meaning they found in life, into these stones."

Her words hung in the air, mingling with the temple's timeless quiet. She glanced at Yen, catching the awe in his eyes. For a moment, they stood in silence, side by side, immersed in the profound stillness of a history that seemed to transcend time itself.

Later, they found themselves in the shadow of an ancient stone arch in a fort. It stood tall against the clear blue sky. Yen, stepping back to get a better view, tilted his head upward. "Look at how perfectly it frames the sky," he said, his voice thoughtful. "It's like the vastness of the world captured within the boundaries of our perception."

Anya, captivated by the scene, raised her camera and snapped a picture: Yen's silhouette, small against the monumental arch, the sky stretching endlessly beyond. As she lowered her camera, a quiet smile played on her lips. "Maybe we all want to leave something behind," she mused, her tone contemplative. "Something bigger than ourselves."

Yen turned to her, caught off guard by her words. He studied her for a moment before nodding slowly. "Yeah… Maybe it's about trying to experience something beyond ourselves, too."

That evening, as they gathered around the dinner table with Ranee, they eagerly shared the highlights of their adventure, showing her videos and photos.

"It was amazing," Anya said, her excitement evident. "I imagine that back then, artisans were like the software engineers of today – the most popular profession." Her comment drew laughter from everyone.

Ranee nodded thoughtfully, scrolling through the pictures. "I must explore the city again! You two have captured it from a perspective I've never seen."

Yen sighed, leaning back in his chair. "I'm completely smitten by all the art we saw today. Back then, beauty was a priority, and culture was quite literally etched into everything. Today, our buildings are just so… linear. And dull. Cold, too."

Anya smiled quietly at his exasperation.

Their conversation flowed late into the night, drifting from the elegance of ancient sculptures to the evolution of art across eras. It was a night of wonder, connecting the past and present through their shared love of creativity.

Early the next morning, the three of them prepared to leave for the wedding venue. As Anya walked into the living room, she paused for a moment. Yen, dressed in a crisp kurta, looked effortlessly charming, his boyish grin adding to his allure. She caught the way his posture subtly shifted when she entered the room, the way he stood a little taller.

He likes the way I look too, she thought, *feeling a flutter in her chest.*

This wedding romance is bound to spill over into whatever we have; she mused nervously. *How are we supposed to keep things simple for the rest of the trip?* The thought tugged at her heart, a mix of yearning and apprehension. She remembered all too well the ache of her last heartbreak. Was she ready to risk that again?

Across the room, Yen stole a glance at her, his thoughts mirroring hers, but in a completely different way. *Why aren't we taking this further?* he wondered, his mind replaying the moments they'd shared – the easy laughter, the shared silences, the growing connection that felt so natural. *We've had such a good time together. What on earth are we waiting for?*

His resolve hardened. *I'll ask her about it tonight,* he decided, his heart both hopeful and uncertain.

They arrived at the venue just as the bride was being brought in by her family. She was radiant in an off-white sari paired with a rich purple blouse and adorned with gold jewelry. Her large, kohl-lined eyes sparkled with excitement. Perched in a decorative cane basket, she clutched the edges tightly, casting nervous glances at her older uncles as they carried her towards the groom.

Yen couldn't help but laugh when Anya and Ranee began mimicking the bride's cries of mock protest as her uncles playfully pretended to stumble.

Later, as the bride and groom exchanged symbolic gestures – placing a mixture of cumin and jaggery on each other's foreheads to signify a commitment to weather both the bitter and sweet moments of life together – Anya's eyes glistened with emotion. Yen noticed his chest tightening as he watched her.

I could do that with Anya, he thought, the idea taking root with surprising ease. *Although, I doubt there would be much bitterness between us.*

The rhythmic hum of the priests' chanting filled the air, weaving a sacred spell over everyone present. The couple's evident intimacy seemed to carry the entire gathering into a collective dream – one of love, hope, and the possibility of something timeless.

The ceremony surrounding the tying of the auspicious thread was filled with pure joy and reverence. As the priest chanted his slokas, a relative nearby explained the significance of the vows being made. The groom tied three knots as he secured the turmeric-coated thread around his bride's neck. It represented that they were now one in thoughts, speech, and action.

The symbolism of the moment was profound, reaching beyond the couple at the centre of it all, spreading among the onlookers. Each person, touched by the depth of the promises being made, reflected on their relationships and what they longed for within them: connection, trust, and the commitment to journey through life together.

Anya and Yen decided to head back to Ranee's home after the wedding lunch. A relaxed lull followed – "lunch-induced stupor", as they jokingly called it. Weddings always seemed to have that effect.

When Anya woke up in the early evening, she was surprised to see a bouquet of fresh flowers at her door. As she stared at them, Yen appeared, holding two cups. "I made us some coffee," he said casually, through the soft music playing in the background.

Stepping into the living room, Anya noticed he had set up a small table with cookies and coffee. The cozy atmosphere felt oddly intimate. Yen gestured toward the table, "Come," he said, his tone serious and deliberate, "There's something I've been meaning to talk to you about."

Touching one of the flower petals, she looked at him, "Yen," she asked, her voice tentative, "Did you… buy these flowers for me?"

"Yes, I did," he replied, his eyes searching hers. "I hope you like them."

"Yes… yes, of course, I love them!" she stammered, momentarily caught off guard by his earnestness. *Why did I say love? I could've just said like*, she thought nervously, and then, *what am I trying to fight here?*

Taking a deep breath, Yen stepped closer and gently took her hands in his. "Anya, I know you've wanted to keep things simple between us," he began, his voice steady but heartfelt. "But I've never felt this close to anyone before. You're funny, smart, beautiful, and strong. I never thought I'd find someone like you. I just - I like being with you."

Anya's heart raced as she became acutely aware of his hands holding hers. She looked up, meeting his warm gaze, "Me too, Yen," she said softly, relief and happiness flooding in.

That was all the encouragement he needed. He leaned down and gently kissed her, the moment dissolving the tension that had lingered between them for days.

The evening became theirs, a quiet celebration of their new connection. When Ranee returned later that night, she found them sitting cozily on the couch, watching a movie together. "The wedding seems to have had a ripple effect!" she teased. "Do you need just one bedroom from now on?"

The days that followed felt like a song to Anya and Yen. Time flew as they explored the city, took countless pictures of each other, and spent their nights entangled in shared laughter and whispered conversations.

Yet, amidst her happiness, Anya couldn't stop a thought - that this was just a fleeting romance born out of proximity and shared experiences. *I hope it isn't,* she thought. *But the rest of our trip is going to be so much more interesting*! Smiling, she looked at Yen who was trying to get the perfect light for a photograph of her.

Their next adventure – a beachside resort in the Lakshadweep Islands – felt perfectly timed. With the new turn their relationship had taken, it promised to be a journey neither would ever forget.

INSIGHTS

> *"Love never dies a natural death. It dies because we don't know how to replenish its source."*
>
> **– Anais Nin**

Love needs to be nurtured, just like a garden with flowers. It has to be cared for and tended according to its nature. Different plants require different types of attention, and in the same way, different people require different ways of being loved.

Do you know what makes you feel loved? And, as an extension, do you know what makes your partner feel loved?

It's interesting to observe how Anya and Yen's relationship evolved. They started as friends, but when romance entered the picture, their dynamic changed in so many ways. It brought in a unique kind of emotional and physical intimacy and a deep sense of attachment.

Romantic love feels like a euphoria inducing drug. It can be compulsive and overwhelming in the first stages, it even makes one believe in destiny. Later on though it is an active choice! You don't get it simply by virtue of birth and unlike friendships, family ties, or even parent-child relationships, a couple stays together by choice.

You're signing up to share almost everything, from the mundane-ness of daily life to major life events, from the quietly comforting routines to the painfully unstable times. It's a commitment to face life's challenges as a team, ideally, in sync with each other's thoughts, speech and actions. It isn't inherited or forced but like friendships; it's crafted, maintained, and, nurtured.

Romantic relationships also come with their own unique set of expectations. As partners, we want companionship, someone to talk to regularly. We ask for unconditional emotional support in times of turbulence. We expect that our partners will share our values, and desire the same lifestyle. When conflicts pop up, we find it incomprehensible that our partners think so differently and want them to agree with us. We want to be able to take them for granted. When these huge expectations aren't automatically met, love is questioned.

Understanding Love

A great book for understanding how to love someone consciously is *The Five Love Languages by* Gary Chapman. I highly recommend giving it a read! While there's some debate about whether it's comprehensive, it certainly sheds light on the fact that everyone gives and receives love in different ways.

In the book, Chapman identifies five distinct "love languages": gifts, words of affirmation, quality time, physical touch, and acts of service. He stresses the point that we have to understand the way our partner feels loved and love them in that way. Love is effort, if your partner feels it differently from you. When two people want to express love, they have to learn and understand each other's love language rather than continue to speak in their own language.

For instance, have you ever felt that you are trying so hard to show your partner that you love her but she doesn't seem to feel it? Well, that's the key message from Chapman's book: we all have unique ways of feeling loved. While the concept is easy to grasp, it can be hard to practice. While this might seem a little unnatural at first, it teaches us to pay attention to our partners' needs.

On the other hand, when one is "in love" all this seems so easy. In fact, we then tend to speak all of the languages. There is delight around buying gifts, messages praising the other, eagerness to be relevant and useful to the partner, and a constant desire to touch. Not to mention the fact that any free time is used to connect with one's partner. When this phase fades, then building a long-lasting love requires an effort that is directed correctly.

"Attention to the uniqueness of your partner is the bedrock of any relationship!"

Just like a bodybuilder works on building a strong, healthy body, a relationship needs daily practice and dedication.

Tanu and Varun found themselves puzzled about what was going wrong in their relationship. They both professed love for each other but they weren't feeling that love. Varun's job required him to travel frequently, and he always made it a point to bring back gifts from his trips, hoping these tokens would show Tanu that he was thinking of her. Even when he shopped for himself or hung out with friends, he ensured he picked something –small or big, for her. Tanu, however, told him several times to stop spending money on unnecessary things since they were saving up for a car. During one heated argument, she even questioned whether he thought he could buy her love, and if he thought gifts would make up for the time he spent away from her.

Varun expressed his frustration at this, wishing Tanu would stop asking for so much of his time. He wanted her to understand that, like everyone else, he only had 24 hours in a day, and he felt limited in how much time he could dedicate to her. Varun pointed out that they already spent time together going to movies, partying with friends, and visiting family, so he couldn't quite grasp what more she wanted from him.

When Tanu explained that she wanted some quality time at home with just him, possibly a dinner together, doing an activity, or even simply chatting about life, Varun was taken aback. He wondered how much more they needed to talk and learn about the other; they did get married because they knew each other well after all.

The crux of this situation is that they hadn't learned to speak each other's love language!

For Tanu, gifts didn't convey love, while for Varun, quality time didn't seem important.

Building Love

If it's not organic, in the long run, then we need to build it consciously. So what is conscious love? It is not head-over-heels infatuation. It definitely is not blind or a feeling of emptiness or neediness. Instead, it is love that is rooted in awareness and mindfulness. While there is no doubt that the initial rush of falling in love is intoxicating, for a relationship to thrive in the long term, it needs to evolve through attention into conscious love.

> *"Given the complexity and attachment in a romantic relationship, it would be very unrealistic to think it will flourish organically."*

Building love consciously involves three factors:

Firstly it needs self-awareness. A partner can trigger to the surface all the deep rooted beliefs, fears and patterns that were kept suppressed. It is not uncommon to feel surprised at who one can become in a relationship. Only when I know myself well can I know another well. Knowing yourself comes before loving yourself or anyone else.

Secondly, there is an awareness of your partner. They too have deeply seated beliefs, fears, and patterns of behavior that is etched into their psyche. When you are able to see what they are, it will become clear that their behavior in the relationship is not because of you. This makes it easier to empathize and problem solve.

Thirdly, it requires an awareness of the effort. Consciously loving someone is a living and dynamic experience, a journey over time rather than a start or an end. Mistakes happen in all relationships, either committed or omitted, but with conscious love, there's room for change because there is an effort in that direction.

In a nutshell, conscious love is about being aware, taking responsibility, and actively working on your relationship – every single day. It's neither easy nor the well trodden path.

Activity Time

A MAPPING QUIZ

Goal: to see how aware you are of your partner.

Here are some questions for you and your partner to answer separately. The answers are either yes or no, but if you say yes, feel free to elaborate a bit.

Once you've both completed your lists, share your answers and have fun discussing how well you did. Perhaps this will suggest future date night activities.

- Can you name at least one of your partner's best friends?
- Do you know your partner's favorite type of cuisine?
- Do you know your partner's favorite way to relax after a long day?
- Are you aware of your partner's favorite type of music?
- Do you know the type of alcohol (if any) your partner prefers?
- Can you recall your partner's biggest goal in life right now?
- Are you aware of any fears or anxieties your partner has?
- Do you know the name(s) of your partner's parents?
- Do you know your partner's favorite book or author?
- Can you name a skill or hobby your partner is currently trying to improve?
- Are you aware of your partner's stance on the current educational system?
- Do you know your partner's views on religion or spirituality?
- Can you name a significant event or memory from your partner's childhood?
- Do you know your partner's preferred way of showing affection?
- Are you familiar with any dislikes or pet peeves your partner has?
- Do you know your partner's favorite holiday or festival of the year?
- Are you aware of your partner's favorite movie or TV show?

- Do you know something your partner considers to be their biggest achievement?
- Are you aware of a goal your partner has set for the future?
- Can you name something your partner would never want to do or try?
- Do you know any of your partner's current personal or professional aspirations?
- Are you aware of your partner's favorite sport or physical activity?
- Do you know how your partner likes to dress?
- Are you familiar with a value or belief that is very important to your partner?
- Do you know a travel destination your partner has always wanted to visit?
- Do you know what your partner finds most attractive in a partner?
- Do you know if your partner has any boundaries when it comes to physical affection?
- Are you familiar with what makes your partner feel most desired or loved?
- Are you aware of your partner's needs or expectations around the frequency of intimacy?
- Do you know if your partner has any past experiences that shape their views on sexuality?
- Are you aware of whether your partner enjoys romantic surprises or gestures?
- Do you know your partner's approach to budgeting and saving?
- Are you aware of your partner's biggest financial goals or dreams?
- Do you know if your partner has any current debts or financial obligations?
- Are you familiar with your partner's preferred approach to managing shared expenses?
- Do you know how your partner feels about credit cards and borrowing money?

- Are you aware of any financial habits your partner wants to change or improve?
- Do you know your partner's comfort level with discussing finances openly?

> *"Love because you have discovered that someone that is good enough to make a part of your permanent life"*
>
> **– Elle Sommer**

Takeaways from This Chapter

Use this space to jot down your thoughts and responses. This is an important concept for relationships and you might enjoy reading your insights later on!

Me

Do I show love to my partner and make them feel cherished? How do I tend to show love?

My Partner

When does my partner feel loved? How do they try to show me love? How can I express my love for them through actions and effort?

Our Relationship

What are the habits we can develop to ensure we are mindful of each other's language of love and be nurturing toward each other?

CHAPTER 7

TRUST

The sky had turned a stunning shade of orange, muted yet brilliant. As the sun dipped below the horizon, the ocean shimmered, the landscape transformed into something almost surreal – like a photograph come to life.

"I wonder who came up with the name Lakshadweep," Anya said, "It means a hundred thousand islands, but in reality, there are only thirty-six."

"Maybe someone got lost trying to find the island they were heading to," Yen joked. "Frustrated by all the wrong turns, they just called it Lakshadweep." Then turning to her, he asked, "Are you happy we came here for your beach experience?"

"I'm delighted, Yen – both with the trip and with us," she said, smiling and leaning in for a kiss.

"Now, I can see a thousand stars," he laughed, his eyes twinkling with the light of the setting sun.

Anya pulled back slightly, still mulling over the trivia, looked at him, and said, "The islands were named fairly recently, you know- no more than fifty years ago."

Unwilling to let the romantic moment pass, he pulled her back, "I'm officially naming you my distraction," he said.

As they turned to head back to their resort, they bumped into another couple also on vacation.

"Anya!" exclaimed the man, his face lighting up. "Fancy meeting you here!"

"Hi, Randy," Anya said, looking shocked, "Surprise indeed!" She smiled and gave him a quick hug.

"Yen, meet Randy," Anya introduced them. "We were in college together. And Randy, meet Yen, he's a friend."

Randy introduced his girlfriend, Uma, saying, "Uma, meet the lovely Anya – she was the one to turn to during our angst-filled college days." He turned back to Anya with a grin. "It's been ages! Let's catch up for old times' sake?"

Anya hesitated, her mind briefly flickering to the past. Should I let the past be where it belongs? She thought, and then said, "We've got tomorrow all planned out already."

"Oh, come on!" Randy pleaded. "Uma loves meeting people from my past. She says it helps her see me in a different light," his tone was light-hearted.

Uma, looking a little curious, spoke up. "You haven't mentioned her before. I thought I knew all your friends." She reached out to Anya's hand, adding, "Please, let's meet tomorrow. I'd love to hear your stories."

Anya glanced at Yen, who shrugged slightly, indicating he didn't mind.

"Alright, let's set it up in the morning," Anya said, looping her hand into Yen's and turning to leave. "Have a good night!" she said, smiling at Randy and Uma.

"Randy seemed to be into you," Yen remarked later that night, his tone casual. "Were you two close back in college?"

"We dated for a bit, Yen," she replied, her voice quiet. "For about eight months. It didn't end too well. That was six years ago."

Yen looked at her carefully "Tell me more."

Anya sighed, leaning back. "We were part of a group of seven friends – three girls and four guys. We were tight-knit, all trying to earn our degrees. Randy was a bit of a party boy."

Tucking her legs under her and holding a pillow, she went on, "It was during the last year of college that Randy and I got closer, and became more than friends. It made us grow a little apart from the rest of the group. There were a lot of fun times – parties, drives, movies – but soon I got tired of it. I wanted to focus on my studies, to make sure I had a good future. When conflicts started over our different priorities, he started partying with another friend of ours from the group. Eventually, they were hanging out more than he and I were, and it ended up in a pretty complicated breakup."

She paused, her eyes distant. "Young love can be fun, but it's also kind of blind."

Yen leaned in with an uncertain look in his eyes. "Hmm. Should I be worried?"

"Not at all, sweetheart," Anya smiled, giving him a tight hug. "It's a memory, but it means nothing. I love what I have with you."

Yen chuckled. "I wonder what stories we'll hear tomorrow," he said.

Anya raised an eyebrow. "Are you sure you want to have dinner with them? We can call and cancel if you're uncomfortable."

He shook his head, reassuring her. "It's okay. I'm good with it."

They spent the next day learning scuba diving, an experience that emphasized the importance of knowing their equipment and trusting both the instructor and each other. They were preparing for a unique challenge – a nighttime dive to witness the bioluminescence of the coral reefs.

At dinner, they met Randy and Uma at the resort. Randy and Uma were dressed sharply. Yen and Anya, tanned from the day's diving lessons, had opted for a casual look.

When Randy heard how Anya and Yen had met, he grinned. "Where was this Anya hiding during college?"

Anya laughed, "You were so wild back then, I had to compensate by being wary."

Uma raised an eyebrow, clearly surprised. "So, you two were pretty close back then?"

"Oh, we even dated for a bit, Uma," Randy said dismissively.

Uma looked taken aback. "You didn't think to tell me about that?" Her tone was tinged with surprise and anger.

In the silence that followed, Yen squeezed Anya's hand gently under the table, taking the edge off the tension. "Do you want to tell them about our scuba diving bloopers? Or shall I?" he asked, shifting the conversation to lighter, safer ground.

She looked at him relieved, and said laughing, "Yen couldn't see a thing underwater at first because he forgot to put anti fog on". Soon, everyone was talking about the weirdest things they had ever done.

The next day was spent training for the night dive. Although the thought of diving into the ocean at night was intimidating, they felt confident in their instructor's abilities. As the time approached, Anya realized how difficult it was to rely completely on someone else when visibility was so low. The ocean, pitch black and much cooler than during the day, now seemed a little scary.

Yen checked in with her. "How are you feeling, Anya?"

"Excited but nervous," she replied, trying to hide the unease in her voice.

After completing the pre-dive safety checks and understanding their limits with depth, they were ready to go.

"You will see a completely different ocean at night," the instructor said, his voice reassuring. "Let's have a good time!"

As they dove in, the water lit up beneath them. The bioluminescence in the ocean made every movement set off a shimmering glow. The darkness of the night dive was in stark contrast to the brightness of their torches, illuminating glittering coral, curious turtles, colorful sea creatures, and the occasional startled fish.

They had just started to relax into the rhythm of the dive when suddenly, Yen's torch flickered and went off. He momentarily lost his bearings, and Anya panicked. Her heart raced, but she quickly collected herself, as she saw him swimming toward her for help. The instructor, who had noticed the issue, came to their side almost immediately, helping Yen get his torch working again.

Despite the brief scare, it was an incredible experience. Anya and Yen returned to their room, both happy and silent.

"I'm glad we did that together, Yen," said Anya.

"Yes, it's amazing what goes on in the world that we don't know about. So many different species thriving together in such a well-coordinated way! Being human and experiencing all this is such a gift too," Yen replied thoughtfully.

"What about the dive struck you the most?" Anya asked.

"I guess it was how we could all rely on each other to enjoy something so fascinating," he said.

"What about you, Anya?" Yen asked.

"I think it was seeing a whole different world in a whole different way. It's wonderful how everything coexists. There are so many ways to be," she replied.

They lay in bed holding hands, each lost in their thoughts before drifting off to sleep.

The rest of their time on the islands was spent exploring, meeting new people, sampling the freshest fish, and collecting stories from the islanders. As they did so, they grew more attuned to being a team, learning new ways to complement each other. Their time there seemed to flow by very quickly.

Their next stop would vastly differ from the beach vibes of Lakshadweep – Chettinad, famous for its food and architecture.

"I guess beautiful mansions and spicy food will make for a completely different experience from the laidback, slower pace of the islands," Anya mused as they packed for their next adventure.

INSIGHTS

> *"Whoever is careless with the truth in small matters, cannot be trusted with important matters"*
>
> **– Albert Einstein**

Einstein is not talking about honesty here, but integrity. Being careful with the truth means that our intention is aligned with our behavior. One might act with the best of intentions, but trust comes from being that way even in small matters.

Take Anya and Yen, for example. Anya was respectful of Yen's feelings and shared important information with him. In return, Yen was honest about his emotions. On the flip side, Randy tried to reassure Uma that his past with Anya didn't matter, but the fact that he hadn't mentioned it earlier raised some doubts. Not being careful with small matters made him seem untrustworthy. Uma could easily wonder what else he might be hiding.

Understanding trust

Have you ever stopped to think about how much we rely on trust in our everyday lives? Trust is at the heart of pretty much everything we do. For instance, we trust that when we flip a switch, the lights will come on. We trust in the rhythm of the seasons, the daily rotation of the Earth, and the ebb and flow of the oceans. We trust that if we plant a seed and take care of it, it will become a tree. It's like trust is etched into nature.

Such trust comes from the fact that these things happen consistently and there has never been a reason for us to doubt it.

In society, we trust so as to be functional. We trust that if we show up to work and do a good job, we'll keep our jobs. We trust that the justice system will protect us from harm. We trust that the food we eat every day doesn't contain harmful chemicals. It could easily be proven a delusion, but we continue to trust because it serves us to do so.

In our personal lives, it's slightly different - trust is more fragile because it includes hope. We trust that the person we choose as our partner will be loyal to us. We trust that our friends will stick by us when times get tough and that our children will care for and love us when we're old. We even trust that we'll wake up the next morning. So even when trust is based on hope, it's vital to normal functioning in life.

This is why it is such a big deal in relationships - It is the foundation upon which the relationship rests. Trusting your partner means that you can rely on, be sure of, and believe that they are true to you. With it, you can be your authentic self and without it, life would become unpredictable and unsafe.

Trust can be blind or smart depending on how much you have thought about your partner, your goals, and your inherent desire for it. When it is given to someone freely, it is not an act of courage or love, but of ignorance. When it is withheld without reason, it is not wisdom but fear.

Building Trust

So, how do we build trust in our relationships? I believe it is a three-pronged approach.

- Firstly through **integrity**: When what you say aligns with what you do and resonates with how you feel, you can be relied upon. Integrity also has to do with being consistent.
- Secondly, through **care**: When you are involved in your partners' wellness and are interested in their lives, you are automatically leaned on.
- Lastly through **openness and vulnerability**: This allows your partner to truly understand and see you for who you are. This intimate knowledge fosters trust and intimacy between the two of you.

Building trust takes effort. Sometimes we stumble, but if we reflect on our relationship with these three lenses, we can figure out what went wrong and work to fix it. Trust doesn't have to be a precious commodity to be given only if there's perfection; it can include room for errors and imperfections, allowing relationships to be sustained.

Rebuilding Trust

Trust can be destroyed in so many ways - not just through infidelity, abuse, or major betrayals, but also through those smaller, everyday actions that often go unnoticed. Actions like sharing private details without consent, hiding smaller financial issues, or using hurtful language can quietly chip away at the foundation of trust.

With the smaller breaches, there is compromise - especially if the overall value of the relationship feels worthwhile. In those moments, couples recognize that trust can involve perseverance, acceptance, and patience - just as much as it involves fidelity and loyalty. It's this intricate dance of give-and-take that keeps relationships alive and thriving.

However, when there has been a serious breach like infidelity, abuse, and deceit, it might require professional intervention.

Typically the process begins with the acknowledgment of the wrong, even those aspects that haven't been explicitly stated. There is a tendency inherent in us to deny or suppress what is painful. But rebuilding trust is a painful process where you learn not to justify or ignore or hide what the reality of the situation is. It calls for humility from both partners and involves moving from apologizing, to atoning for the breach. It can take a long while before the couple can learn to feel attached again.

This is best done with therapists who are equipped to handle such situations because they are a neutral party intent on helping you to rebuild your trust. Be careful about trying it on your own. It can spiral out of control because you are an involved party.

> Ben had a gambling addiction that he had hidden from his wife, Stella. She was a homemaker and they had three small children. Ben earned a decent income that could easily cover all their expenses. Given this, Stella couldn't understand how they ended up with no money at the end of the month and no savings at all.
>
> She noticed large sums being withdrawn regularly and when asked Ben explained that he needed to pay off some loans he had taken out earlier. Stella expressed gratitude for not having to worry about money.
>
> Then one day, some unsavory people showed up at their door asking for Ben, claiming that he owed them a lot of money. Alarmed, Stella asked Ben what was going on. He assured her it was all under control and told her he needed her support. She was very happy to do so.
>
> Stella finally decided to seek help when Ben lost his job because he had borrowed money from his colleagues. In therapy, Stella started to understand her codependence was as serious as his addiction.
>
> Together as they worked on their issues, both as individuals and as a couple, they understood that the relationship would stand only with strong determination and compassion. Getting past the deceit, manipulation, and recklessness they had allowed would take a lot of time and effort. But they put certain strict boundaries in place, committed to being in therapy until recovery, and made a "no exceptions" plan around work and money. While doing this, they decided that Ben would work on getting back his career and Stella would handle their finances.

Activity Time

CASE ANALYSIS

Here's a small story for you and your partner to discuss. See if you can pinpoint the values that were compromised and led to the breakdown of trust. Then, think about what the couple in the story might do to rebuild that trust.

Anita and Vikram had been happily married for over five years. They were a compatible team, effortlessly managing their shared home and supporting each other's careers. They often bragged about their unbreakable relationship, and their friends even called them "couple goals."

However, the first cracks began to show when Anita, who usually handled their finances, dipped into their savings to invest in a risky venture without consulting Vikram. When he found out and confronted her, she said she didn't want him to worry about the details. But Vikram was shocked that she took his trust for granted. He wouldn't have said no to her idea; it was the fact that she made this decision without telling him, that made him feel insecure.

Tensions rose as Anita struggled to understand why he was upset. She saw her decision as something that would have benefitted them. To avoid confrontations, Vikram started working late but started wondering if all his hard-earned money should just be handed over to Anita. His absence unsettled Anita, and when she tried to ask him about it, he shut down and retreated even more. One evening, when Anita confronted him, he snapped back, asking why it mattered to her since she didn't care about how he felt.

Anita hadn't realized just how much Vikram was struggling with what had happened. She had downplayed the impact of her actions and their arguments. Not knowing how to handle the situation, she decided to wait out the conflict, but this only strained their relationship further.

Their conversations became superficial, and they grew increasingly silent around each other.

Then one day, Vikram decided to confide in a mutual friend. When Anita found out, she felt betrayed and asked him why he found it easier to talk to someone else instead of her. He replied that he didn't think she wanted to understand, but that she only wanted to defend herself.

Eventually, they both admitted that their relationship had become fractured and decided they needed to work together to mend it.

What do you think? What values were compromised here, and how might they start rebuilding trust? Discuss this together. Then try answering the following questions to gauge your trustworthiness.

Self-Assessment for Building Trustworthiness

1. Do I honour the personal thoughts and feelings shared with me?
2. Do I follow through on the promises I make to my partner?
3. Do I respect my partner's boundaries without pushing or challenging them?
4. Do I avoid speaking negatively about my partner when they aren't around?
5. Do I listen attentively and value the perspectives of my partner?
6. Do I handle disagreements calmly and respectfully, without escalation?
7. Do I share important information openly with my partner, without waiting to be asked?
8. Am I supportive of the goals and ambitions of my partner in the way they need support?
9. Can my partner count on me to be present and reliable when they need me?
10. Do I take accountability for my actions and apologize if I have caused hurt?

11. Do I show a genuine interest in the well-being and happiness of my partner?
12. When I make a mistake, do I make a sincere effort to correct it?

Each "Yes" response reflects a positive behaviour that helps build trustworthiness. On the other hand, any "No" answers point out areas where there's room for improvement and gives you insight into how you can strengthen trust in your relationship.

This questionnaire is designed to encourage self-reflection on how your actions align with being a trusted partner, friend, or family member. Keep in mind that it's not exhaustive; it's just a starting point to kick off your introspection.

> *"Man's life would be wretched and confined if it were to miss the candid intimacy developed by mutual trust and esteem."*
>
> **– Edwin Dummer**

Takeaways from This Chapter

Any journey that is inward needs time and space for self-reflection. Use this space to jot down your thoughts and responses.

Me

How do the concepts brought up in this chapter apply to me?

My Partner

Does my partner feel comfortable relying on me? How do i feel about trusting my partner?

Our Relationship

What are the steps we can take to build and strengthen mutual trust?

CHAPTER 8

CONFLICT RESOLUTION

Massive mansions and stately heritage homes lined modern streets – a striking contrast to the beachside paradise Anya and Yen had just left behind. They had journeyed from a realm shaped by nature's hand to one crafted by human artisans. The salty sea breeze of Lakshadweep still clung to their senses as they stepped into the gentler, earthy warmth of Chettinad.

Where Lakshadweep had been a canvas of open skies and endless, deep blue horizons, Chettinad enveloped them in a tapestry of rich, earthy tones and architectural grandeur. The small-town bustle blended seamlessly with the aromatic embrace of spices, while the whispers of history hung heavy in the air, carrying tales of wealthy merchants and vibrant traditions.

Anya and Yen strolled hand in hand along the sun-dappled streets, marveling at the grandeur of ancient homes. The ornate facades of the mansions spoke of painstaking craftsmanship, each intricate detail a testament to the devotion of its builders. A friendly local, noticing their curiosity, guided them toward a mansion that welcomed visitors.

Crossing its threshold was like stepping into another time. The corridor before them was lined on either side by gracefully carved wooden pillars, their intricate designs on the base and head. The air carried a heady blend of jasmine, camphor, and sandalwood, an aromatic homage to Chettinad's cultural richness. Yen's eyes lit up as he pointed to the ceiling, its patterns complementing the elaborately carved wooden panels adorning the walls. Each panel seemed to come alive – narrating tales of a bygone era.

"I wouldn't want such art in my house," said Anya, wonderstruck. "It would be overwhelming! However, those large framed windows would be so perfect."

"I rather like the idea of a reading room," Yen mused. "Walls covered in murals, maybe a pillar or two to lean against while reading."

Their laughter spilled over as they imagined their ideal homes, agreeing that beauty mattered, but realizing how differently it could be defined. Yen slipped his arm around Anya and said, "Maybe we'll have a house together someday."

Anya stiffened briefly before deciding to laugh it off. "Let's not build castles in the air now!."

"Haha - I hope you're not saying that 'cause I'm just going to be a travel fling!" Yen remarked, his tone turning slightly serious. *I really, really hope I'm not* he thought.

"Well," she replied, smiling, "seeing how time is so different now than earlier, maybe this is our version of a time-travel romance." *I hope Yen doesn't rush things* she thought.

They laughed as they imagined the quirks of time travel and its endless possibilities. Yet, beneath the jokes and easy companionship, they both felt the quiet weight of their unspoken differences.

After some shopping and a little too much walking, they returned to their countryside villa, letting warm embraces soothe away any differences as they settled in for the night.

The next morning, Anya wore a stunning red Chettinad-style cotton sari. Her loosely tied bun, red *bindi,* and delicate earrings gave her an elegant charm that left Yen mesmerized by how effortlessly she transformed her look.

Their day's plan was to visit a temple famed for its terracotta horses. Located on the edge of a serene village by a simple pond, the temple was a delight of vibrant colors. However, Anya couldn't proceed beyond a certain point due to traditional restrictions on women and had to satisfy herself through the photos Yen took for her. Out here, the painted ceilings and the rows of terracotta horses kept her occupied. Anya found herself deeply fascinated by the devotion and beliefs they represented.

Yen caught up with Anya as she stood by the terracotta horses and pointed to a nearby tree adorned with bangles.

"It's a tradition," she explained. "Women tie bangles there, hoping for good life partners."

"What do you feel, Anya?" Yen asked. "Is it about finding the 'right' person or about making it work together?"

"There's no simple answer," she replied.

Yen hesitated, then said earnestly, "I feel like we get along so easily, Anya. I look forward to traveling more with you, meeting your family, and introducing you to my friends."

Anya smiled and teased, "Is this the part where I say, 'Hold your horses'?" snapping a picture of Yen with the terracotta horses. "Let's not rush, Yen. Our relationship is still new. Let's focus on the present."

"So...you aren't very sure about us," Yen asked, his voice tinged with hurt. "I like you, Anya, and I guess I just assumed we were on the same page."

"No, Yen," she said gently. "I like you too. The pace I move at is just different. I'm at a point in my career where I need to make big choices. I can't just rush into something right now."

Yen nodded, though the disappointment lingered. "Maybe we're spending all of our time together and it isn't giving you time to reflect," he said. "Why don't we take a day to explore Chettinad on our own? We had fun doing that before, right?"

Anya recognized his retreat but agreed. "Sure. It might be a good idea."

Yen's need for reassurance weighed on her. She understood that Yen, who came from a broken home, might crave security- but she was feeling rushed.

They had lunch with the villa's owners, and the meal did not disappoint - Chettinad cuisine, famed for its bold flavors, lived up to its reputation. Yen kept the conversation lively, sharing anecdotes from their travels, earning smiles and laughter all around.

After lunch, Yen turned to Anya. "I'm heading out then. I'll see you tonight."

Our first fight, Anya thought, watching him leave. *And like most conflicts, it's about expectations.* She sighed, unsure how to feel.

Yen returned late that night, tiptoeing into the room. Anya, feigning sleep, didn't stir. *The talk can wait until later,* she thought, her mind swirling with the weight of unspoken words.

The next morning, Yen was gone before Anya woke up. A note by her bedside read: "Have a wonderful day. Back by dinner."

After a delightful breakfast of *idiyappam* and stew, Anya spent the day exploring. She wandered through local markets, marveling at bold wood carvings, unique baskets, and weavers crafting signature Chettinad *saris*. Renting a cycle, she toured the town, visiting mansions and a palace, and interviewing locals to uncover the histories of their families, and finished the day feeling fulfilled.

Meanwhile, Yen had hired a driver and ventured to nearby villages for a more offbeat experience. He visited a workshop specializing in the handmade tiles that Chettinad was famous for, delighting in the craft.

Later that night, they met for dinner. Yen had bought her a beautiful *Tanjore* painting of a dove. He placed it on the table between them.

"It represents peace and love – a keepsake from our time here," he said, taking her hand. "I want to … you know… make peace."

Anya's gaze softened as she admired the painting, its delicate stones placed perfectly to enhance beauty. "Thank you, Yen," she said warmly. "It's beautiful."

They sat down on a courtyard bench, and had a long talk about their perspectives on relationships. They spoke openly and sorted out their differences - carving a shared understanding.

"I see now that we're moving at different paces," Yen said finally. "And that's okay – it doesn't mean anything other than that we're different."

Anya nodded. "We're figuring this out as we go, and isn't that what matters?" She rested her head on his shoulder.

Yen smiled contently. He was glad that they came to this conclusion, not with grand promises but with genuine and mutual intentions that they both wanted to honor

INSIGHTS

> *"Never let a problem to be solved become more important than a person to be loved."*
>
> **– Leo F. Buscaglia**

When we realize that our conflicts have shifted from figuring out what's causing the friction to figuring out who is causing it, it's a sign that we're in trouble.

Have you ever wondered why we struggle so much with conflicts in our relationships, even though we hear time and again that they're inevitable?

If conflicts are so integral to relationships, shouldn't we have learned to handle them better? During a conflict, we get emotionally charged and lose sight of all the good and happy moments built up during peaceful times in the relationship. Is it possible then, to navigate these ups and downs without feeling overwhelmed? Absolutely! But it requires some effort and understanding.

Take Yen and Anya, for example. They have very different approaches to life:

- Yen is all about security and affirmation, eager to discuss their future together. Anya, on the other hand, values her independence and prefers to be more cautious, taking things slow.
- Yen dreams of pursuing their goals together as a team. Anya, instead, wants to have her own space and ambitions.
- Yen is clear about the direction of their relationship and wants to take the next steps, while Anya prefers to let things unfold naturally without being bound to a strict timeline.

At first glance, these differences may not seem so impossible or likely to lead to much conflict. However, it's small issues like these that escalate because underlying values don't fully align. The key to reconciling these differences lies in accepting them rather than judging them negatively. For instance, Yen can give Anya the space she needs, while Anya can reassure Yen of her commitment to nurturing the relationship. They could also have an open conversation about what commitment means to each of them, using that understanding to strengthen their bond.

With a shared intention to nurture their relationship, there are plenty of ways for them to bridge their differences and keep growing together. Embracing each other's perspectives can lead to a deeper connection and a healthier partnership overall.

> *"When the intention is to keep a relationship, there are a myriad of ways to do so."*

The Role of Expectations in Relationships

Expectations have been given a bad rap and the consensus is that we should avoid having them. But we all do. I have heard a lot of people say that one must not have expectations. That in itself is a huge expectation, is it not?

The reason we get into long-term relationships is that we expect to be each other's support and companion. Conflicts usually arise from differing expectations.

When asked about expectations, the usual answers are loyalty, support, love, boundaries and effort. These are **fair expectations**. If not for these, why would we want to be in a committed relationship? However there are also the **little expectations** that cause everyday conflict that add up over time.

The expectation that your partner will intuitively understand if you are upset or that they will pick up the slack at home if you are running late- even if you haven't told them, or that they will give you attention whenever you need it are examples of the little ones. The expectation that they will fulfill all your expectations is a **big expectation**.

It is important to clearly differentiate between what has been clearly articulated versus those that are silently held in the mind - an **unvoiced expectation**, is inherently an assumption.

We all come from different backgrounds, grew up in contrasting circumstances, and therefore have differing expectations and desires. But isn't that perfectly okay? The key point to focus on is that conflicts can arise from not verbalizing these differences. To have a harmonious partnership, we need only learn how to do a reality check!

Addressing Root Causes of Conflicts

Although conflicts stem from various issues, we often focus on surface triggers rather than deeper causes. For example, imagine a couple who are arguing about how much time one person spends on their phone. The real issue could be underlying feelings of neglect or insecurity. This can intensify and turn into an insurmountable difference if they're only going to talk about the phone itself. Resolving such a conflict cannot be done by just setting limits on screen time.

Getting to the underlying emotion is hard to do if there are a lot of issues. It is then best to go to a therapist. However, if the relationship is doing well, you can uncover these emotions through curious questioning.

Constructive Conflict Resolution

Conflicts can be both destructive and constructive, and the outcome depends on how we address our disagreements. All of us are aware of their destructive nature. Many of us develop ways of coping with conflict that can add to the problem. Some fight back, others stay silent. Some sulk and others use humor. If couples have learned to handle them constructively, the key lies in the word "Learned".

Relationships are complex and multifaceted, and therefore, conflicts within them rarely have simple solutions. How we handle conflicts directly impacts the longevity and health of our relationships. When we approach conflicts in a non-threatening and respectful manner, we are able to come out of these disagreements with greater intimacy and understanding.

Unhealthy conflict involving blame, retaliation, contempt, and suppression damages relationships. These patterns of behavior develop early on in life, and frequently, we remain unaware of them.

I won't try to list all the different causes of conflict because that would be impossible. However, when we dig down to the core of most conflicts, we often uncover similar underlying issues—feelings of helplessness, powerlessness, fears of rejection or abandonment, and a sense of worthlessness or uselessness.

That's why in couple therapy, individual sessions serve as the foundation. This allows each person to address their core issues before coming together to explore how those issues affect their relationship.

There are different conflict resolution strategies and each couple must explore them to discover what works best in their situation.

Sheila and Jai came to therapy because they were constantly fighting about household chores. Sheila expressed her frustration, saying that she did not want to subscribe to traditional gender-based roles in their marriage. She wondered why her doing the chores was an assumption while he only stepped in when asked. Jai responded by pointing out that he earns double her salary, and while she keeps most of hers, his income supports both of them. He asked if that wasn't also a form of gender expectation.

Sheila feels that the chores becoming her responsibility is due to her being a woman, while Jai believes that providing for his partner is just what men are expected to do. Even though they are a modern couple who reject gender stereotypes, they find themselves caught in those very roles. Both are accusing each other of hypocrisy. What Jai hears isn't the issue; it's the blame and labels being thrown around, and his retaliation only serves to make Sheila look hypocritical. This creates an unhealthy conflict that feels threatening and disrespectful. The couple is divided – the separateness causes the conflict.

Instead of going down this path, Sheila could have simply said, "Let's make a plan for the chores because I feel like I'm shouldering most of the responsibility." Jai could have replied, "We also need to talk about our finances and figure out what we want as a couple."

Activity time

CHECK MATE or check with mate!

Here's an exercise to help you understand conflict better. Choose two different problems to discuss: one, a local community issue or an environmental concern and two, a problem in your relationship. For the best results, record your discussion and keep it to 15 minutes. Follow these steps for each topic:

- **Set Ground Rules**: Agree on what makes a safe space for your conversation. Establish rules for conflict, like no yelling, name-calling, or ridiculing.
- **Use a Timer**: Make sure each person talks for no more than two minutes at a time.

Discussion Steps:

1. **Identify the Problem Together**: Clearly and specifically define what the issue is.
2. **Share Your Perspectives**: Talk to each other about why the problem is causing stress and share your views on it.
3. **Communicate Understanding**: Before replying, express what you've understood from your partner's perspective.
4. **Aim for a Win-Win**: Work together to find a solution that benefits both of you.
5. **Reflect on Successes**: Identify what went well in your conflict resolution process.

You'll likely notice differences between how you handle the two scenarios. Discuss these differences without letting emotions take over, and see what strategies work best for you.

While these steps may seem straightforward, it can be hard to grasp completely and needs detachment and patience. An experienced third party – like a therapist could help.

> *"The words of the tongue should have three gatekeepers: Is it true? Is it kind? Is it necessary?"*
>
> **– Proverb**

Takeaways from This Chapter

Any journey that is inward needs time and space for self-reflection. Use this space to jot down your thoughts and responses. I have added some questions to help with this.

Me

How do I handle conflict? Does it help or harm my relationship? Do I avoid, escalate or negate conflict?

My Partner

How does my partner handle conflict? What can I do to de-escalate conflicts?

Our Relationship

What are the ways in which we can handle conflict as a team rather than as opponents?

CHAPTER 9

COMMITMENT

"Just two more places to go, Yen," Anya said, a hint of sadness in her voice. "After that, it'll be back to our normal life."

Cupping her face in his hands, Yen smiled. "Now that we have each other and all these memories, maybe our new normal will be even better, and I'm looking forward to that," he said.

"Me too," she said and then wondered, "A stable, committed space... Will we handle that as well as we've handled this fun, exciting phase?"

"I think that'll be the better part of our relationship. Sometimes I just need to feel secure more than anything else," Yen replied. *I've become rather open and vulnerable,* he thought, remembering his fears of being found superficial. *And it's all because of Anya.*

"Is this hug secure enough?" she joked, holding him tightly. "I have grown to love the spur-of-the-moment adventures and unplanned moments – the kind you're a master of!" she added.

Being together had become easy; they enjoyed each other's company without pretenses or fears. Walking outside their room amidst the beautiful lawns, under a crescent moon that lit up the Kerala landscape, and talking about life seemed so natural now.

"I'm so excited to see the Theyyam," Anya said, referring to the ritualistic art form where the performer is believed to be possessed by the deity that he is depicting through dance and storytelling.

They were in Kannur, a coastal town in Kerala known for its beaches and handlooms.

"Did you see that movie called Kanta – I didn't know about such inspired and passionate rituals until I saw it there. I've been waiting to see it in person ever since," she said.

"I loved that movie too – it gave me goosebumps," Yen replied. They discussed it at length and then read up about the Theyyam performance.

As they were having dinner that night, Yen got a phone call that seemed to rattle him.

"I'll be back in a moment," he said, standing up hurriedly. "Eat up before the food gets cold."

He was gone for quite a while, and Anya decided to return to their room. When she opened the door, she was surprised to find Yen already there. He was packing his things.

"What's happening, Yen? Why are you packing your bags?" she asked, concerned.

"I'm sorry, Anya. I have to leave. You may have to finish the trip on your own," he said.

"This is so sudden. What was the call about?" she pressed.

"I'll text you, but right now I need to go," he replied. "The cab's here. I'm going to miss you," he added, giving her a quick peck on the forehead before leaving.

Anya stood frozen, shocked. *Why couldn't he take a minute to explain?*

He didn't even send her a text earlier when she was waiting for him at the restaurant. Confused and angry, she ran after him, but his cab was already gone. Her mind raced with questions, torn between anger and concern. She went to bed still agitated, sure that he would have sent an explanation by the next morning.

When Anya woke up, the first thing she did was check her phone for a message from Yen. *Nothing.*

It was a beautiful room with a lovely view of the river by a waterfall. As she sat mulling over what had happened, she decided that she would spend the day at the hotel, enjoying the room and going to the spa. By noon, however, she was upset and had texted Yen.

"Is everything okay Yen?" she asked.

His reply was brief: "I'm fine."

Yes, but I'm not, thought Anya. *And he doesn't seem to care about that.* She wondered if this erratic behavior would be a pattern in their relationship.

The next day, Anya decided to explore the city and its beaches. While she engaged with the sights and met some interesting people, a dull ache lingered in her chest. She couldn't shake feeling horrible that Yen had left without explanation.

An hour later, 30 kilometers away, she realized she was so distracted that she had left her phone at a restaurant. Fortunately, the restaurant called her hotel – they had her phone and would deliver it the next day, but for now, it would just be her and her camera.

It felt strange to be without her phone, surrounded by strangers. She felt completely alone in the crowd.

Perhaps I should just marry my phone, she thought. It comforts me almost as much as Yen does. Independence had always been empowering for

Anya, but she now realized there was certain sweetness in dependence too.

That night, she stood at the edge of the crowd, camera in hand, watching the Theyyam performance. The rhythmic drums reverberated in her chest, but her thoughts were still with Yen. His abrupt departure had shaken her. *What kind of commitment were they building if he could just vanish without a word?*

As the performer danced, possessed by a deity, oblivious to his surroundings, Anya wondered, *Can I lose myself like this – trusting, hoping, and giving myself to Yen? Is that what it takes to be in a relationship?*

After capturing enough footage for a great vlog, she returned to the room, exhilarated yet exhausted. As she fell asleep, her last thoughts were of the acceptance she had found with Yen, and how it had allowed her to embrace their differences.

Early the next morning, she went to visit a homestay run by a couple she had met the previous day. They had hoped she would feature them in her vlog. She was impressed by the care with which their home had been adapted for guests. It showcased local artwork, coffee table books highlighting the beauty of Kerala, tree houses, swings, and the most delicious food. She promised them that she would return. She missed Yen terribly and was eager to get her phone back that evening.

When she checked her phone, she saw that Yen had tried calling multiple times and sent worried texts asking if she was okay. That night, she called him back.

"Anya, are you okay?" Yen asked. "Why weren't you answering my calls?"

"No, I'm not okay, Yen," she replied, tears rolling. "You have a lot of explaining to do."

"Can I explain when I meet you?" Yen asked.

"Well, you seemed to have made that decision on your own when you left," she retorted.

"I'm sorry, Anya. Perhaps you'll understand when I explain," Yen said.

"Perhaps," Anya replied, trying to sound cold.

"Will you extend your stay by a day?" he asked. "I can reach tomorrow evening, and we can go to Pondicherry together."

"No, Yen," Anya said firmly. "I'll leave for Pondicherry as planned and will see you there if you're still coming."

"Please, Anya, let me come and explain," Yen pleaded. "I swear, when you didn't answer my calls, all I could think was that you were breaking up with me."

Anya hesitated, thinking, *If I give in, will I set a precedent for similar behavior in the future? Is this something I want to accept?*

"I'm sorry, Anya," Yen said. "I realize that it wasn't responsible of me to go away like that."

Anya softened. "Alright, Yen. I was just so confused when you left without explaining."

They agreed to meet the next evening at the hotel.

Anya spent the day at a *Kalari* school, learning the basics of the ancient martial art native to Kerala. The founder shared how intense the training was and how perseverance was the key to mastering it.

Anything worth the name has its time of trials and perseverance, she mused. *Perhaps Yen's perseverance will make tonight a good one.*

When she returned to the hotel, Yen was already there. A bouquet and a box of her favorite chocolates sat on the bedside table, and Yen was fast asleep. Not wanting to wake him, she quietly moved to the balcony and sat reading for a while. Eventually, Yen stirred and called her name.

"Anya," he said, "Come here and give me a hug – I've missed you so much."

She should've held back, but before she knew it, she was in his arms, saying, "I missed you too."

A few amorous moments later, they sat up, with Yen holding her hands.

"I'm sorry, Anya. I should've explained earlier," he said.

"It's true," she replied, "but I'm all ears now, Yen. What happened?"

Yen hesitated, looking vulnerable. "I was afraid of how you would see me if you knew about what happened … about my father."

Anya looked at him seriously. "You can't protect me from the truth, Yen. If we're going to be in a relationship, you have to let me choose."

Yen's mind was racing as he spoke: *I hope this doesn't cause us to break up. Will Anya stay after how I've behaved?*

He took a deep breath and said, "I come from a rather unstable family, Anya. I had to learn not to depend on, or involve anyone."

He paused before adding, "The call was from my mom. My dad was arrested for fraud. He borrowed a large sum for a business venture that failed. Under pressure from investors, he sold off his last asset – land – and gambled with the money, hoping to recover his losses. But things only got worse. Instead of being transparent and facing the situation, he went into hiding. Someone filed a complaint, and the police tracked him down."

Yen's voice trembled. "I was shocked when I got the call, Anya. All my anger at the instability my dad caused throughout our lives came flooding back. I couldn't think clearly. My mom asked me to come immediately, and I thought I could explain it to you later. I realize now that rather than avoiding the truth, being transparent would have been better."

His head hung low, the weight of the situation pressing on him. Anya stayed silent but reached out to hold his hand, offering him comfort without saying a word.

They sat quietly for a while, the darkness setting in as the day ended and the lights flickered on. The quiet comforted them both, giving space for reflection.

"I understand that you were confused, Yen," Anya said softly. "It must have been quite shocking to hear all of that over the phone. I hope everything got sorted out."

"Mostly, yes," Yen replied. "We found him a good lawyer, and he's been talking to his partners and friends, asking for time to figure out a plan." He paused, his voice quieter. "I don't want to be like him, Anya, but I'm afraid I might be."

"Oh, Yen," Anya said, her voice warm and reassuring. "Awareness is the first step to overcoming any compulsive behavior. Our actions lie with us, even if our thoughts sometimes aren't our own."

Yen looked at her, gratitude and relief filling his expression. "That's so profound, Anya. You're right – I lost myself there for a bit."

He then softened, his gaze turning to her. "It must have been shocking for you too, Anya, to see me leave like that without any explanation. Thank you for letting me come back and explain."

Anya sighed. "Yes, it shook me," she admitted. "I didn't know what to think. It made me wonder if what you said about us getting serious was true. It made me spiral, and I felt insecure. In the future, I just need you to tell me at least the crux of the situation, in brief, so I know what to expect."

Yen felt a pang of guilt, realizing he hadn't been sure if he could open up to her. He hadn't wanted to risk losing her. But in the end, it was his silence that had almost caused that.

"I love you, Anya," he said, his arms enveloping her as they got ready to head out for dinner. "You are the best thing that has happened to me."

Anya grinned, teasing, "Ooh, the L-word made its presence felt! Isn't that supposed to be a big turning point? Have we turned?" She laughed, hugging him back, adding, "I love you too, Yen."

Later, as they lay in bed, Anya's thoughts drifted. *I hope Yen's fear of being like his dad won't make him overcompensate and stifle what could be a free-flowing relationship.*

Yen, meanwhile, pondered the complexity of responsibility. *Dad was trying to be responsible but in a reactive way. Maybe his fear of losing face was just like what I felt with Anya. What I saw as instability might have just been desperate attempts to overcome failure.*

Both were left to wonder about the future, but for now, they had each other and a sense of companionship that felt like stability.

INSIGHTS

> *"The man who wants a garden fair, Or small or very big, With flowers growing here and there, Must bend his back and dig."*
>
> **– Edgar A. Guest**

A poet can express something so ordinary in such a profound manner. While most of us know desire, achieving success involves commitment. Guest's key message here is that desire needs to be backed by effort and dedication.

Anya rightly ponders whether commitment would be easy with Yen. While Yen longs for it, his actions sabotage his desire. Both Yen and Anya are learning that commitment isn't just a feeling; it's a conscious ongoing choice.

When couples first commit to each other, the emotional charge is high. It becomes easy to overlook the hard work it will mean to maintain a relationship. In the throes of love, it can be hard to imagine that what feels effortless now could become challenging later on. While emotional commitment may bring two people together, it's practical commitment that keeps them together.

Commitment requires perseverance, faith, and a willingness to fully embrace another person – even when you don't fully understand them.

The Commitment Conundrum: Are We Afraid of Forever?

The word "commitment" has become quite intimidating when it comes to relationships. The idea of sticking together for a lifetime can feel scary, and it's easy to understand why. Many of us haven't seen inspiring examples of marriages or long-term relationships. Divorces are very common, frequently messy, and relatively easy to obtain. There's also the fear of being stuck in a dead-end relationship. In today's world filled with opportunities, the fear of missing out on someone or something better can hold people back from committing. At its core, commitment raises the question: What if I'm making the wrong choice?

So what does commitment mean? Does it mean staying together no matter what boundaries are crossed or promises broken? Does it mean remaining together even if the basics of a romantic relationship aren't met, as long as there's friendliness and comfort? Does it mean managing finances jointly, even if one partner isn't responsible with money?

I have had clients come to therapy wondering if they have to live without sex, financial security, or even a home because their partner isn't interested in those things. They feel committed to their marriage but struggle to resolve these significant differences and feel stuck.

Priya and Rohan had been married for ten years, but cracks in their relationship had grown wider over the past two years. They were finding it hard to talk to each other without slipping into blame and conflict. Priya felt like she was carrying the weight of their relationship on her shoulders. She wondered what had happened, especially since Rohan had been so involved in the beginning. On the other hand, Rohan was feeling exhausted. He worked hard to provide a comfortable life for them and didn't like feeling pressure when he returned home. He didn't know what else he needed to do.

One day as they were talking, Priya broke down as she shared a specific example of why she was feeling so disheartened. Rohan had promised to fix the dishwasher weeks ago, but nothing had happened. Eventually, Priya took it upon herself to fix it. She told him that it had become such a pattern in their relationship that more often than not she didn't ask him for help. She wondered why she was the only one solving problems around the house. She went on to say that they had made a commitment to their life together and not just to love.

Rohan was shocked by her perspective; he had assumed she had everything under control. Priya too had a job to go to, but he had let her shoulder all the responsibilities of the house. In that moment, he realized that he hadn't been committed to addressing practical issues because he had prioritized his work over hers. He had also assumed that love and good intentions would be enough to keep their relationship going.

When Priya explained that she would feel supported if he helped with responsibilities and tackled problems as a team, Rohan agreed that commitment meant more than just loyalty and love – it also involved actively participating in their life together.

The Practical Art of Commitment: More Than Just a Promise

Practical commitment feels like work because it is! But it is work that is worth it in the end. After all, a meaningful and lasting relationship comes with effort.

What does commitment feel like in practice? It means doing what you promised to do and giving your time and energy to fulfill the obligations you made to your partner. It means being dependable and prioritizing your partner, for example, by taking time off to care for them when they're sick, or by stepping in to help with their responsibilities when they're feeling overwhelmed or tired. It means being inclusive and making plans keeping their choices in mind and being loyal, choosing to stay true to them and not just physically.

While the exact definitions can differ for each relationship, acting on what commitment means to you as a couple ensures that your relationship remains relevant.

Navigating Relationship Challenges to Nurture Commitment

Challenges are inevitable in any relationship. When people from different backgrounds come together, differences in beliefs and habits can create some friction. What seems cute at first can quickly become frustrating. For instance, a partner's indecisiveness might be charming initially, but it can get annoying when you find yourself making all the decisions. Or those playful jokes that once made you laugh might start to feel negative or condescending over time.

How one responds to these frustrations is the key to making a relationship work. It might be easier to shut down or get defensive, but it takes open, honest, and collaborative communication to move past challenges. When couples see difficulties as chances to show commitment instead of reasons to pull away, they build trust and create a stable relationship. That's what commitment is all about – it takes perseverance!

Commitment is also built by creating shared memories. You've probably heard the saying, "A family that eats together and plays together, stays together." These daily shared moments become a ritual of commitment. So, commitment isn't just a milestone to reach; it's the ongoing effort you put in to keep what matters most to you strong and thriving.

Activity Time

THE I DO JAR

Create an "I do" jar for each of you, where you both put in notes about small or big actions of love and support that you can do for each other. Here are some examples of what you can put in your jar:

- Leave a sweet note for them to find.
- Help with a chore they dislike.
- Plan a surprise dinner or picnic.
- Give them a relaxing foot massage.
- Send a thoughtful text in the middle of the day.
- Offer to take care of something on their to-do list.
- Plan a date night
- Revisit a memorable time.

Add to this list every time you hear them wish for something simple. You could also ask them for what they would like from you and add that to the jar. Have at least a hundred notes before you start acting on them.

Pick one note from the jar each day or once in two days and do what it says.

Set aside time each week to reflect on what actions made you feel stronger about your relationship

Celebrate Your Growth: At the end of the week or month, discuss how these efforts have strengthened your bond.

This simple practice fosters love, appreciation, and growth in your relationship.

"There's a difference between interest and commitment. When you're interested in doing something, you do it only when it's convenient. When you're committed to something, you accept no excuses."

– Kenneth Blanchard

Takeaways from This Chapter

Any journey that is inward needs time and space for self-reflection. Jot down your thoughts and responses. Use the questions as a guide.

Me

How well am I able to commit to the relationship? Do my actions show my partner that I am invested in us?

My Partner

In what ways do I want my partner to show commitment to me? Am I able to discuss this?

Our Relationship

What are the habits we can develop so that we can keep our relationship active and thriving?

CHAPTER 10

INTIMACY

The final destination of their journey was Pondicherry. As they cycled along the streets with French names and colonial-looking buildings, they stopped occasionally to look at the colorful graffiti splashed on walls. Cascading bougainvillea spilled out from every nook and corner, enhancing the old-world charm of the cobblestone pathways.

"How seamlessly South Indian culture blends with French influences here," mused Anya, taking in the unique ambiance.

"It's such a distinct vibe compared to all the other places we've visited," Yen said with a smile. "I like it!"

They stopped often to get photos and videos of the streets and the vibrant walls imbued mostly with different shades of yellow and orange. As evening approached, they decided to cycle along the beach road, eventually dismounting to have a meal at a cozy beachside café. Listening to the rhythm of the waves, they sat together in companionable silence, watching the flickering candles on their table dance with the breeze.

The café's owner approached them with a warm smile and a leather-bound book in hand. "Would you mind signing this?" he asked politely.

"What's it for?" Yen inquired curiously.

"I've been maintaining this for about two years now," the owner explained, introducing himself as Carl. Taking a seat nearby, he opened the book to reveal pages filled with photos and heartfelt notes.

"Every day, I invite someone visiting the café to sign this book and share what made them stop here. Initially, I thought it might help with reviews, but over time, it's become something more – a collection of stories, memories, and moments that I hope to turn into a book someday," he said with evident pride.

Anya and Yen leafed through its pages, captivated by the tales of love, loss, dreams, and reflections left by previous visitors. The entries painted a vivid tapestry of human connections. Adding their own story of adventure to its pages made them feel like they belonged with a group of strangers – all connected through this little café by the sea.

Anya wrote: "This café marks the last stop of an adventurous journey we began as strangers. Traveling together and meeting so many different people has brought us closer in a way we never imagined. Tonight, sitting here and writing in this book has been not only romantic but deeply insightful. I'm grateful for places like this that remind us how connected we all are."

Yen added: "I've found someone I never want to let go of. Writing together in this book feels like a beautiful way to connect with all who've been here before us and all who will come after."

That evening, the laid-back charm of the city offered a welcome respite from the whirlwind of emotions and adventures that had defined their travels.

"What a lovely day this has been," Anya murmured, stretching lazily across the bed before sinking into its embrace. Speaking into the pillow, she asked, "Been quite a hot day. Ready for bed, Yen?"

"Not quite, Anya," Yen replied with a mischievous grin, his fingers tracing a slow, teasing line along her legs.

She turned her head, smiling playfully as her eyes roamed over him. Moving slightly to make room, her voice grew softer, tinged with invitation. "And what are you thinking of?"

He met her gaze as he shrugged off his shirt, leaning closer with a smirk. "about more hotness to keep you awake!"

Her laughter mingled with the distant murmur of the waves, filling the room with a warmth that mirrored the intimacy of the moment – a perfect end to their unforgettable day in Pondicherry.

They were up early the next day, dressed in loose-fitting cotton clothes and wide-brimmed hats, their skin generously slathered with sunscreen. Their first stop was the Promenade Beach to catch the sunrise, savoring the cool morning breeze and the serene hues of dawn. Later, they wandered into a quaint French bakery, eager to indulge in crepes and buttery croissants.

Yen, unable to resist, ordered nearly every pastry on display, savoring each bite with exaggerated delight. "This is heaven," he declared between mouthfuls.

Anya chuckled, rolling her eyes at his indulgence. "Yen, you're hopeless. At this rate, we'll need to hire a cab just to carry you home!"

Their next stop was at Auroville, an Ashram boasting a unique residential community of people from different nationalities. It was built on the principles of simplicity and spiritual growth, as taught by Sri Aurobindo. The lush landscapes and meditation centers were tranquil and inviting, and they were intrigued by the extensive libraries. While exploring, they were invited to join a discussion group on Sri Aurobindo's teachings.

Anya and Yen found themselves on opposite ends of the philosophical spectrum during the discussion.

"It's all well and good to delve into spirituality, but not if it means ignoring the world's pressing problems," Anya argued.

Yen leaned forward; his eyes alight with conviction. "But he's not talking about escapism – it's about gradual transformation. If humanity could evolve spiritually, we might actually solve those problems at their root."

Anya shook her head, her skepticism evident. "That sounds lovely in theory, but don't you think it's overly idealistic? Reality doesn't pause for us to retreat into mystical realms."

"Maybe," Yen countered, "but what if that very transformation is the key we're all missing? Dismissing it as idealistic could mean overlooking a real solution."

Their debate continued over a tantalizing vegan lunch; the flavors of the food, however, did not get lost in the intensity of their conversation. The afternoon unfolded in a plethora of ideas – spirituality versus practicality, idealism versus realism – each defending their perspective with passion, yet listening with interest.

With their appetites sated, Anya and Yen made their way to a potter's workshop to try their hand at the wheel. What had seemed effortless in the hands of the skilled potter quickly revealed itself as an art that demanded patience and precision.

Anya stared in mild frustration at the lopsided clay bowl she was trying to shape for Yen – it was the third time it had collapsed under her touch. Meanwhile, Yen's attempt at a candle holder for her looked more like the whimsical creation of a third-grader. Their shared exasperation soon gave way to inspired shopping, as the potter, amused by their struggles, guided them to shelves displaying his ready-for-sale masterpieces.

With newfound respect, they bought a couple of well-designed planters as keepsakes.

"Will we grow plants together, Anya?" Yen asked, examining the planter with a smile.

"I hope we do much more than that," she replied, her laughter bubbling up in response to his earnestness.

Yen grinned. "Let's celebrate this 'plan for a future' tonight. I've heard about a great lounge not far from where we're staying. My dance moves could use some polishing."

By late evening, they were back in Pondicherry and heading to the dance lounge. Promising a playlist filled with nostalgic hits from the '80s, it was a place Yen felt sure would have the perfect vibe.

When he extended his hand, inviting Anya to dance, she hesitated, not confident. "You go ahead," she said, almost shouting over the pulsating music. "I'll just sit and watch. I've never really been out dancing before."

"No way," said Yen, mouthing his words to get over the loudness, "It's time to get groovy and silly!" He struck a goofy pose, and Anya laughed at his dramatics.

Without giving her a moment to refuse, Yen pulled her onto the dance floor. Amid a sea of colorful lights and infectious beats, her initial awkwardness melted into carefree joy. They stumbled over each other's feet, laughing at their clumsiness, but relished the closeness of moving together in sync with the music.

When the DJ started taking song requests, Yen's enthusiasm spilled over. His knowledge of the '80s hits revealed a playful, nostalgic side of him that Anya couldn't help but adore.

"This was such a wonderful day," Anya said, slipping off her shoes as they strolled back. "The most 'us' day till now."

Yen smiled softly, draping an arm around her shoulders as she leaned into him, her arm wrapped snugly around his waist. The night air was cool and salty, and the gentle sound of waves accompanied their quiet steps along the moonlit beach.

"So, what's next?" Yen asked, his voice low and content.

Anya looked up at him with a smile, her eyes reflecting the glimmer of the ocean. "more of us," she replied.

Together, they walked on, the beach stretching ahead, filled with the promise of shared adventures to come.

INSIGHTS

> *"This is intimacy: the trading of stories in the dark."*
>
> **– Elizabeth Gilbert**

This paints such a beautiful picture –two people in the dark, not seeing each other, yet so relaxed in the security of their connection, they share their stories. It's easy to get wistful hearing this because it is what we all seek: someone to be totally at ease with.

Intimacy is a beautiful experience! It happens when someone can enter our inner and personal space with ease, and we don't feel unnerved at all. It takes courage because we know that this kind of vulnerability will either save us or break us. Either way, we grow when we experience it.

Take Anya and Yen's journey in Pondicherry. Their experiences reveal just how layered intimacy can be. They've shared wild adventures, heated debates, and even some hilarious failed attempts at clay modeling. Even the simple act of dancing together becomes intimate when they let go of their inhibitions.

In the early days of a relationship, passion creates an electric intimacy. But as that fire calms down into something deeper and loving, a tender intimacy starts to grow, something easy and comfortable. We begin to see our partners for who they truly are – not just the idealized version we've created in our minds. Sometimes, it takes commitment to kindle intimacy; other times, intimacy ignites commitment.

Nurturing intimacy – the delicate thread

Think of intimacy as a delicate thread binding two people together, creating an "us" from a "you" and a "me." But if not cared for, these threads can fray. However, when layered, they grow quite strong.

It's easy to think the honeymoon phase will last forever, but anyone who has been in a relationship knows that magic can disappear just as quickly as it appeared. To keep intimacy alive, we need to pay attention – not just to our partners but to ourselves. It's not a default setting; it has to be cultivated and prioritized.

For example, over time, if sex becomes more about satisfying urges than delighting in the other's presence, intimacy starts to fade.

Relationships are work; there's no escaping that. But having an intimate connection is the reward for all that effort. Intimacy becomes both the catalyst and the result of a healthy, thriving long-term relationship,

Beyond the Physical: Understanding True Intimacy

But what is intimacy,? Most people assume it's about how good the sex is, but sexual intimacy can happen without emotional or intellectual connection. In the same way, a mental connection you have with a stranger on a bus can be intimate. Even a friend is someone you are emotionally intimate with.

In a relationship, intimacy has to be created on many levels. A lack of emotional or mental connection

is noticeable in the bedroom because sexual intimacy is profoundly affected by our experiences, emotions, and thoughts.

When couples come to therapy, a lack of positive intimacy is usually at the heart of their issues, second only to poor communication. This erosion happens so slowly that one day you wake up and wonder why you're still with your partner. Career pressures, lack of time, fear of vulnerability, and procrastination become the foxes that ruin the vineyard of your relationship. When intimacy is neglected for too long, life feels burdensome. Our connections with ourselves and others are what make for a full life.

Intimacy is about being seen and being heard and being wanted. When we are truly connected to ourselves – aware of our own needs and desires– we become better equipped to tune into what our partner needs. If you are not whole within yourself, you can't be there for someone else in a way that makes them feel seen and heard. Emptiness within you will seek attention from your partner rather than offer it to them.

Building Intimacy: All the Layers

The meaning of intimacy varies across cultures. In cultures where individuality is valued, intimacy revolves around sharing thoughts, emotions, and experiences, all aimed at creating an "us." In collectivistic cultures, however, "us" is the norm – so intimacy develops from safely discovering the "I" and "you" hidden in the "us." Not all cultures express intimacy in the same way; some prioritize caring actions and shared responsibilities, while others embrace public displays of love. In today's globalized world, each couple has to learn what keeps them feeling intimately connected with their partner.

Intimacy doesn't have to fade with time; it can deepen and become more fulfilling as we commit to nurturing it daily. It begins by understanding what makes your partner feel connected to you and what helps you feel connected to them. Open conversations about how you both want the relationship to be and creating simple everyday rituals that help you reach that shared vision can cultivate a more profound intimate connection.

Intimacy is built in different ways. I have delineated them below so that you may build them on different levels and start to see what works for you and your partner. Keep in mind that these forms often overlap, and this list isn't exhaustive, it's just a starting point.

Experiential Intimacy

When you spend time doing different activities like hiking, camping, or attending workshops to learn new things, you build common memories and a deeper understanding of your partner as they work alongside you. Having joint experiences such as having a baby, celebrating milestones, or buying a home, builds within us a togetherness that we can fall back on. Even negative experiences like going through a financially difficult time, attending a close person's funeral, or going through a health scare brings us closer if dealt with in the right way. As we live our lives, we also experience intimacy from our day-to-day experiences, like having meals together, going on walks, or watching a movie.

Intellectual Intimacy

Conversations around ideas, values, causes, and books allow couples to delve deep into the minds of their partners. When we actively listen to our partners perspectives, we become aware of who they are and who they aspire to be. It is truly amazing to discover the myriad ways a mind works, and becoming aware of your partner's inner thoughts will give you a deep understanding of what makes them tick. Such conversations have a way of garnering respect and admiration, even when heated debating is involved.

Emotional Intimacy

This is a primary need in humans. To have a safe space where you can express your emotions and feelings in a vulnerable way, without fear of judgment or labeling, is a big gift. Romantic feelings grow in power when we share our feelings with a partner, and they in turn listen and empathize with us. Many times, this area of a relationship is neglected because we prioritize other needs. We assume that because we have loved at one point, it won't fade away.

Physical Intimacy

This is not just about sexual intimacy, but also about the power of touch. Hugs, cuddles, and kisses convey love in a way that words cannot. Sex is a big part of this as well. Good sex keeps a couple in a happy place, and its power in a relationship can never be underestimated. With all the access to sexual encounters that the modern day provides, if this aspect of your relationship isn't nourished and kept refreshing, it paves the way for infidelity. Another danger is that you may slip into becoming just friends. While this might sound like a good enough place to be after a couple of years together, most of our deep-seated need for sexual intimacy will likely have us looking elsewhere or at least wishing for what is being missed. One of the most common reasons people come to therapy is that they have lost sexual connection.

I will not go too deeply into the topic here, but suffice it to say that we all have differing sexual rhythms and desires. The sexual passion we have at the beginning of a relationship will not last, and its flames will require fanning. It is important to remember that sexual intimacy is not just about having sex but about being connected through the act of sex.

Spiritual Intimacy

Spiritual intimacy is that which goes beyond just physical existence. It is concerned with one's spirit – the energy that animates and brings awareness to life. While such intimacy could come from shared religious values, it can also stem from shared worldviews and life goals. When you can share with your partner what you want out of life, and vice versa, the connection between you can transcend the mundane.

We tend to forget that death is real. What is most important in human life is to see how it can be lived, and if you and your partner are aligned on this front, it can make for a strong foundation. By weaving intimacy into the fabric of your life together, you can ensure lasting happiness in your relationship – and who wouldn't want that?

Activity time

INTIMATE CONNECTIONS

Here are some fun exercises that will help you to connect with your partner:

- **Experiential Intimacy**: Set aside time each month to try something new together – whether it's a pottery class, cooking a new dish, or exploring an unfamiliar hiking trail.
- **Emotional Intimacy**: Establish a nightly ritual where you share the highlights of your day, both the positive moments and the challenges, with the intention of staying emotionally connected.
- **Physical Intimacy**: Incorporate small gestures of affection throughout the day, like holding hands, greeting each other with a hug, or stealing a spontaneous kiss.
- **Sexual Intimacy:** Try different forms of touch, read an erotic book together or just schedule regular sex.
- **Intellectual Intimacy**: Engage in thoughtful conversations about a book you've both read, a documentary you've watched, or current events like politics and education.
- **Spiritual Intimacy**: Create and share your own eulogy with your partner. It's a powerful way to reflect on life's purpose and stay aligned with your shared values.

> *"Intimacy transcends the physical. It is a feeling of closeness that isn't about proximity but of belonging."*
>
> **– Steve Maraboli**

Takeaways from This Chapter

Any journey that is inward needs time and space for self-reflection. Use this space to jot down your thoughts and responses.

About Intimacy and Me

My Partner and intimacy

Intimacy within Our Relationship

Relationship Wheel – Progress Tracker

Now that you've gained a deeper understanding of the various aspects of relationships and worked through the exercises and insights together, it's time to revisit the relationship wheels you created at the beginning of this book.

Take another look at it and see if your ratings have shifted. Have your perspectives changed as you've learned more about yourself and your relationship? Are there any areas you feel more confident in, or perhaps areas that now stand out as needing more attention?

Now, it's time to reassess and adjust your ratings. This time, work together to update the numbers in a single wheel and then connect them again. Does the new wheel look more balanced and better suited for a long journey now?

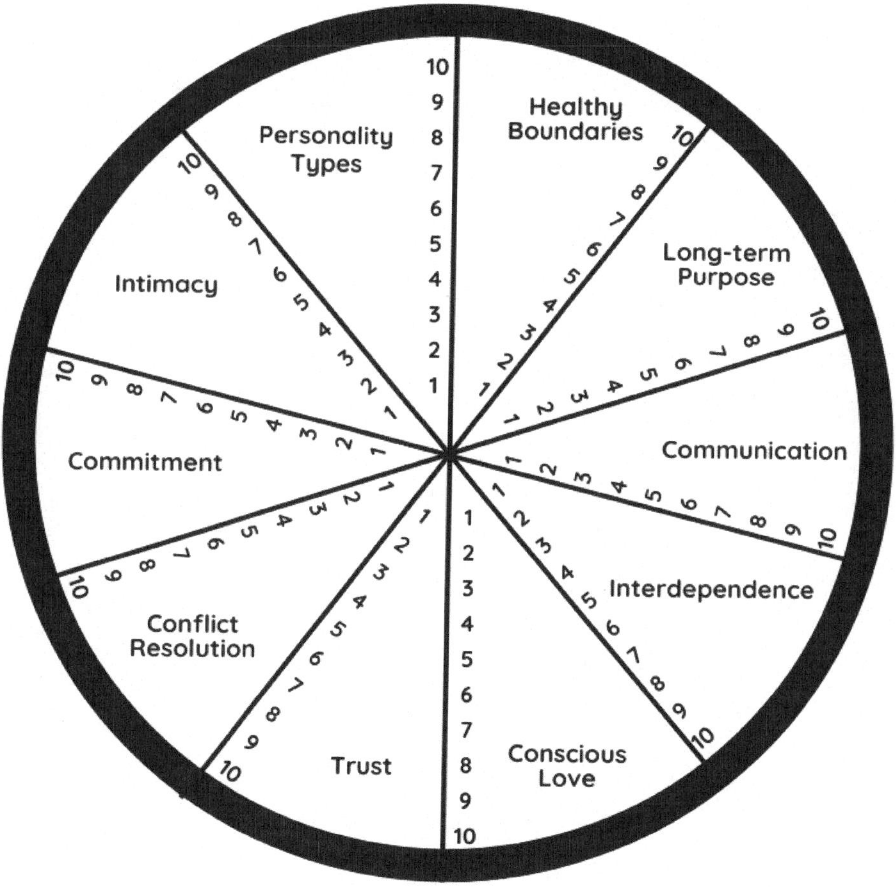
Personality Types
Healthy Boundaries
Long-term Purpose
Communication
Interdependence
Conscious Love
Trust
Conflict Resolution
Commitment
Intimacy
1 2 3 4 5 6 7 8 9 10

Anchoring Your Love

Foundations for a Lasting Connection

Imagine a ship navigating the vast and unpredictable ocean. To avoid going adrift and to brave changes in tide, it needs an anchor. Relationships are the same! Solid foundational principles are essential to staying grounded and navigating life's stormy challenges. Without an anchor, even the most magnificent vessel can drift aimlessly or be swept away by a storm. Similarly, a lack of attention to key elements in relationships can cause them to lose chemistry and meaning.

Relationships, like life, are born of choice, and how well you live and enjoy the relationships you have is determined by these choices. If in making these choices, you have the right tools and mindset; your actions can only create something wonderful. So dream big, but do dream first.

They're so important for our emotional well-being, yet we often handle them without much skill or insight. We take our relationships for granted, thinking we'll get to them after all the "important" stuff in life is done. It's almost like saving the best for last - except when we finally get there, we find out that it's too late for change, and the relationship just continues in whatever state it's been in all along.

Throughout this book, we've been on a journey with Anya and Yen, exploring the different aspects of any relationship – trust, communication, conflicts, intimacy, and more. Now, as we wrap things up, I want to summarize these insights into a framework, brought to life through the acronym – **ANCHOR.**

The last ten chapters act as pieces of a puzzle that address the core elements of relationships and connections. I've tied them all together with the ANCHOR framework, giving you an easy way to remember the key points.

Accept Your Differences and You Become Whole

Acceptance is the cornerstone of a strong relationship. Your partner brings their unique personality, quirks, and boundaries to the relationship. Accepting means that you do not view these as flaws to fix but as differences to cherish. The ideas in the chapters on Personality types and Healthy boundaries explored acceptance of differences in relationships.

Nurture Your Love and Watch Intimacy Ignite

Nurturing love is an ongoing characteristic of a relationship. When we make a conscious choice to invest time and effort into building connection, deeper intimacy is the reward. It's the little things – small gestures, simple words of acknowledgment, and shared experiences that contribute to the growth of your emotional bank account. Love doesn't just sustain itself; it flourishes only when we tend to it with intention and attention. The chapters on conscious love and Intimacy have explored this in more detail.

Clarify The Destination and Communicate The Route

Clarifying what you want in your future together and acknowledging your dreams helps you align your relationship toward that goal. This is best achieved when you can openly communicate any differences and identify all assumptions that could lead to misunderstandings. Keeping an eye on the bigger picture helps you navigate the daily challenges that life throws your way. The chapters on Long-term Purpose and Communication expand on this in more detail.

Harmonize The Individuals and Create The Couple

Harmonizing your unique ways of relating and creating an identity, as a couple, requires an understanding of control. It is about surfing the waves of a relationship by finding the right balance between individuality and togetherness. Just like a beautiful melody comes together when different notes blend harmoniously, a relationship thrives when differences are embraced with understanding and care. This idea was explored in more detail in the chapter on interdependence.

Offer Your Presence and Build a Stable Foundation

When you offer your presence to your partner it creates stability within the relationship. It's about sending the message – through both words and actions – that you choose them every single day. Commitment cannot be just a one-time declaration; it needs to be ongoing. In a relationship, one plus one adds up to so much more than just two! This is explored more deeply in the chapter on commitment.

Reconcile with Vulnerability and Confidence Will Flourish

Creating safety and trust, even when you're going through conflicts, requires vulnerability. When our intentions, words, and actions are in sync, trust flourishes, allowing a safe space for us to explore our differences. Empathy and resilience combine to transform disagreements into opportunities for growth together. The chapters on Trust and Conflict resolution deal with these ideas.

ANCHOR isn't simply a theoretical idea. When your relationship embodies the principles of Acceptance, Nurturing, Clarity, Harmony, Offering of the self, and Reconciliation, it becomes a grounded and secure space from which you can face the challenges that life throws at you. This framework isn't about analyzing your relationship or coming up with fancy strategies. It's all about you – who you are in the relationship and how you approach it.

"The only person you can change is yourself"

Relationships are constantly evolving, mirroring the growth of the individuals within them. Use the principles in ANCHOR as building blocks to ensure that you grow together and not apart.

It's widely known that one of the biggest regrets of the dying is not money, status, or experiences – they're about the people we love most in our lives, and that those relationships weren't nourished enough.

The best relationships flourish in a sweet spot between stability and freedom. "Anchored yet free" sounds like a paradox, but it captures the sentiment perfectly.

Maybe that's the magic we're all looking for in human connections – a balance between being our authentic selves and being flexible enough to nurture the space with others.

"Choose today wisely so that you shape your tomorrow happily."

Next steps:

ANCHOR Workshops

Shared Experiences are like the glue in relationships. Workshops and retreats can be places where both experiences and learning can come together as fun. To that end Anchor your love is also offered as a workshop where you can come over a weekend and have an immersive experience of all that the book talks about. I invite you to take that step to deepen your connection and strengthen your bond.
www.connect-wellness.co.in

Suggested reading:

KHALIL GIBRAN: THE PROPHET

The manner in which he answers questions posed to him, as a prophet, is written in such a beautiful way. This guided me when I was seeking answers.

ROBERT FRITZ: THE PATH OF LEAST RESISTANCE

The idea of creating pathways so that it is easy for energy to flow shaped my thinking in therapy. Addressing resistance to a fulfilled life is the essence of the first few sessions in my practice.

GARY CHAPMAN: THE FIVE LOVE LANGUAGES

It has been such a uniquely useful book when it comes to couples understanding their differences and learning to understand each other.

STEPHEN M.R. COVEY: THE SPEED OF TRUST

Trust is given and earned in different ways in different settings – this book helps to dive into this most important value that holds relationships together.

SUE JOHNSON: HOLD ME TIGHT

Johnson has profound insight into the emotional bonds that couples try to forge. Her book is a must-read for those who want to understand relationships beyond behaviour and rational thinking.

Author Bio

Shree Prabha has spent over 30 years listening deeply—to couples figuring each other out, individuals seeking clarity, and leaders learning to connect with more heart. As a seasoned therapist and founder of Connect Wellness, she blends therapeutic depth with holistic and practical insight in working with modern couples navigating complex relational dynamics.

Before stepping fully into the world of therapy, Shree spent a decade coaching professionals build emotional intelligence and interpersonal competence at work. Her unique blend of experience—across boardrooms and therapy rooms—informs Anchor Your Love: a book designed not just to help couples talk, but to truly understand each other.

When she's not writing or working with clients, you'll find her playing with her 4 adorable dogs, exploring her lifelong fascination with mysticism and inner wisdom or coaxing her plants to life.